Book layout and design: Lynda Gemmell
Cover design & illustrations: John Emberson
Pattern checkers: Mary K. Hobbs and Gayle Bunn
Photography: Leanne Mumford
Technical editor: Deb Gemmell
Contributing Editors: Shirley Scott, Judith Small

First published in Canada by Cabin Fever: June 2007. Second Edition: January 2008.

http://www.cabinfever.ca

email: info@cabinfever.ca

ISBN 978-0-9735657-1-3   Printed in Canada.

ACKNOWLEDGEMENTS

There are always an amazing number of people involved in the production of a book, along with those lending support along the way.

We would like to thank our insightful and encouraging test knitters as they knit and re-knit: Edith Gemmell (our Mom), Bernice Vollick and Dana Gibbons, both also designers for this book. Sophy Cooper, our Shipping Goddess, for cheerfully keeping the orders rolling out the door while we ripped our hair out; our sister Heather for listening while we went on endlessly about the book; to Shirley Scott for her added words and maniacal laughter. And to Mary Hobbs and Gayle Bunn for their careful checking of the patterns. Special thanks to Leanne Mumford, our photographer, for her resourcefulness in getting models into sweaters during the hot summer months; and great thanks to those very warm, but smiling, models.

John Emberson, our graphic artist, and Jim Thomson from Rose Printing, were the only non-knitters (and males) actively involved in the book, but they took great interest, were supportive, and learned how to say things like "stitch definition" so convincingly it almost seemed they knew what they were talking about.

And lastly, to our faithful customers, for their support and their encouraging phone calls wondering when the adult book would be out!

TABLE OF CONTENTS

INTRODUCTION

Welcome to the latest creative product from Cabin Fever. This book is intended to introduce you to the fabulous world of knitting from the top down, this time, for adults.

Our first book, Top Down for Toddlers, first published in 2004, was exclusively for children, aged 1 to 6 years old. A great number of customers asked us for an adult version of the Toddlers book - something for themselves! However, it wasn't just a matter of "sizing up" the sweaters. Structurally, an adult sweater is constructed quite differently from a child's sweater. The Toddler sweaters have no designated front or back (the front neck is the same height as the back neck). An adult sweater fits best with a lower front (or higher back depending on how you look at it), which must be accommodated in the design. Although a square necked cardigan (front neck is the same height as the back neck) with the top button undone accomplishes this objective, we decided to also explore the traditional crew-neck and V-neck styles.

Deb spent endless hours, over the past couple of years, knitting and ripping out, to determine how best to approach an original design concept to deal with the changes needed for adult garments when working from the top down. As always, we try to keep our approach simple and easy to follow and I think you'll enjoy the results of Deb's hard work.

The result is this book of cardigans for adults. You'll see from our photographs that the sweater models are all women. However, there is no reason why a number of these designs could not be easily, and happily, be worn by men. Some minor changes can also be made to keep the men folk happy. See my notes on **Manly Quirks!** page 109.

Three Basic Cardigans in two weights of yarn. Chose to work in DK or ARAN yarn Or try both!

Why are we so taken with the concept of top-down knitting? First, because it fits so beautifully with our design approach: knitting with minimal finishing, and No Sewing! By using circular needles and working the project in one piece there are no pieces to sew together after the knitting is finished. After you cast off the bottom edge your garment is ready to wear.

To introduce you to the concept of top down cardigans for adults Deb designed, sized and tested a set of basic top-down cardigans in both DK (double-knitting weight) and Aran (heavy worsted weight) gauges. The three styles comprise of a square-neck, a crew neck and a V-neck. There are variations on sleeve length and button placement.

We then asked the design team of Deb, Megan, Dana, Karen and Bernice, to have a go at designing their own versions based on one of the basic patterns.

The results are amazingly different. There are easy ones ideal for relatively new knitters or those who've never explored top-down techniques and some have fun and funky approaches with colours, loops and lace to entice the experienced knitter.

We have laid the book out to follow this concept. The first two sections cover the three neck styles of the Basic DK Cardigans and the Basic Aran Cardigans. You pick a neckline, find the instruction box and follow it through the pages.

So please enjoy, and we hope that this book entices you to try a whole new way to knit. If you've already knit from the top down then please sit back, enjoy the designs, and maybe create an original interpretation of your own!

- Lynda

DESIGNER OVERVIEW

Knitting from the Top Down fits beautifully into the Cabin Fever design philosophy of 'minimal finishing'. It also means that the most interesting and tricky part of the sweater is right at the beginning with the neck and shoulder shaping, when you are most excited about your project. It is almost a sweater most of the time you are knitting it—more incentive to finish since it is all together all the time.

I prefer to work from the top down without having to go back and pick up any edges after the knitting is finished. So I wanted to start with the neckband, go into the yoke from there and include the button bands as I was knitting down the sweater. Starting with the neckband was easy and including the button bands was fine but getting a shaped neck was a problem. Although you have a perfectly fine sweater without any neck shaping (the Square Neck here in the book), this limits the knitter to one style. How would I work a Crew Neck and a V-Neck? This took me back to the construction of a crew neck.

If you have ever made a regular crewneck sweater, you know that when you pick up stitches for the neckband you have stitches on your needle from the neck front, back of the neck and the sides of the neck opening. This gives you a neckband with many stitches.

To take that backwards (from the top down), I need to cast on lots of stitches for the neckband and work the yoke somehow to get rid of these extra stitches. A regular type of short row will not work. A short row which would decrease the number of stitches is needed. After making many, many neckband and yoke pieces I have come up with a neck shaping with short rows which accomplishes just this trick. The solution was to use an old short row technique in an entirely new way. It is easy to work and looks good. It is regular and repeating—something I like.

To get down to the nitty gritty: I added 8 stitches (DK) or 6 stitches (Aran) to both Fronts of the Basic Crew Neck Cardigans for a total of 16 or 12 extra stitches on the neckbands. And then worked 16 or 12 Short Rows to compensate for these extra stitches. For the V-Neck, I doubled the number of Front stitches and worked the appropriate number of Short Rows for the extra stitches added. Try it, it works.

I hope you enjoy the Square Neck, Crew Neck and V-Neck versions of the cardigan, with a variation of each worked by one of the Cabin Fever designers. I would encourage you to take this a step further and work out a variation which is truly your own.

- Deb

TO GET A BETTER FIT

Because you are working from the Top Down you have the option of fitting as you work down the cardigan. If you have fitting complaints you can fix them here. A Top Down cardigan can be tried on as you work.

Try It On

Thread spare yarn or a spare needle through sections of the sweater so that it will lay flat. If you use spare needles wind an elastic around each of the ends so you won't lose any stitches. Try on your sweater and see how it fits.

A-LINE OR V SHAPING FOR BODY

To fit myself, I make the bottom of a Long cardigan a little wider than the top. If there is 4"/10 cm or more of a difference between your bust and hip measurements making the cardigan A-line shaped will improve the fit. To add more width to your sweater, on the Body of the sweater increase one stitch before and one stitch after the side seam stitch at both sides of the your cardigan. You can begin 3" below the Divide Row for Body and Sleeve and then continue to increase every 3"/7.5 cm until you have added enough width. You can also start at the waist and add just one or two sets of increases. Every time you work a set of increases you are adding 4 stitches to the width of your sweater. You can be the judge of how much you need.

If you are in the other camp and need to slim down the hips (I envy you first of all) you would work a decrease before and after each of the side seam stitches. I did this for a top down pullover for my husband and it turned out really well.

LENGTH OF BODY AND SLEEVES

I am only 5' tall and always have to shorten every garment I make. This is what attracted me to knitting in this fashion in the first place. I can try on the sweater and check the sleeve length. I can try on the sweater and check for the finished body length. This has improved the fit of my sweaters a lot. If you, on the other hand, are tall you can space out the decreases for the sleeves to lengthen the sleeve. You can of course lengthen the whole sweater too. The beauty of this knitting construction is that you can try it on as you go.

SLEEVES

If you find that your sleeves are generally too snug you can make the sleeves a little wider. When you have reached the total number of stitches for the yoke, you are asked to work 4 to 6 rows without any further increases. You can continue to work increases every other row in the SLEEVE SECTION ONLY of your cardigan to increase the number of stitches for the sleeve.

On the other hand for a slimmer sleeve you can stop working the increases for the sleeve near the bottom of the yoke and continue to work the increases for the Fronts and Back for the correct Body number of stitches. This will give you less stitches for the sleeves and the correct number of body stitches for your size.

Do not change the number of stitches cast on at the underarm. This affects the fit of both the Body and the sleeves.

The sleeves are not difficult to work even when you have changed the number of stitches. Just follow the instructions and ignore the sleeve numbers until you reach the cuff.

REINFORCE THE BACK OF THE NECK

If you are using good sturdy wool this is not necessary. If you are working in soft wool (like a merino or superwash), cotton or if you have very sloped shoulders it would be a good idea to reinforce the back of the neck so it won't stretch out. You can do this after the garment is finished.

With one of your smaller needles and with the wrong side facing, working across the back of neck stitches in the first row of the yoke, pick up & knit one stitch in the purl bump, pick up and knit one more stitch, cast off, continue to pick up & knit and cast off as you go across the back of neck stitches. This makes a slight ridge but it also makes certain that the back of the neck will not stretch as you wear your cardigan.

THREE BASIC DK CARDIGANS

INSTRUCTIONS
FOR THE
THREE DK BASIC
CARDIGANS
ARE ON THE
FOLLOWING PAGES.

FOR THE
ARAN WEIGHT
THREE BASIC
CARDIGANS
SEE PAGES
17 - 26.

THREE BASIC DK CARDIGANS

This Basic DK (double knitting weight) cardigan has three necklines to choose from. There is a Square Neck with no shaping; a Crew Neck with shaping; and a V-Neck with shaping. Options are given on the following pages for cropped, hip or long length bodies along with three sleeve length options.

designed by Deb Gemmell

To Fit Adult Chest Size of:	35" 89 cm	38" 97 cm	40" 102 cm	43" 109 cm	46" 117 cm	49" 124 cm
FINISHED SWEATER SIZE:	39" 99 cm	42" 106.5 cm	44" 112 cm	47" 119.5 cm	50½" 128.5 cm	53½" 136 cm

Materials*: DK weight yarn - 3.5 oz/100g ball, 230 m/250 yds
*Note: The yarn requirements are provided for a wrist length sleeve and hip length body. Short sleeves or three quarter sleeves will require slightly less yarn as will a cropped body. A longer body will require additional yarn.

Main Colour	6	6	6	7	7	8
Ring markers	4	4	4	4	4	4

Needles:

3.5mm/US4 circular needle (24"/60 cm long) for collar and ribbed bottom edge
3.5mm/US4 double pointed needles for cuffs
4.0mm/US6 circular needles in 2 lengths (30"/80 cm long for Body and 16"/40 cm long for sleeves)

Tension:

22 sts = 4"/10 cm on 4.0mm/US6 needle in stocking stitch or needle needed to obtain this tension

NOTES FOR ALL NECKLINES

Please read the following Notes prior to casting on!

1. Knit, or purl, the first stitch of every row tightly to maintain an even edge along the Front Bands.

2. A larger needle is used for the Cast On to prevent the neckband from pulling in. The neckband itself is worked with the smaller circular needle. Set up the Yoke by working the last row of the neckband with the larger circular needle.

3. The neckband, yoke and body are worked on a circular needle, working back and forth. The sleeves are worked on a circular needle in the round.

4. The first and last 4 sts of the neckband will become the Front Bands for the Cardigan. The first Buttonhole is placed in the neckband. For additional options for buttonhole placement see pages 14 & 24.

5. Each Increase Row adds 8 sts to the sweater yoke.

6. Measure the sleeve length from the underarm down to the wrist.

TO BEGIN

The following pattern instructions are divided into the three neck shapings.

Choose which neck shaping you wish to have and follow the boxes with arrows across the subsequent pages.

After the neck shaping is complete, all the cardigans follow the "COMMON ELEMENTS" instructions.

- • **Choose a Neckline Shape;**
- • **Follow the boxes with arrows;**
- • **Move onto the "COMMON ELEMENTS" instructions;**
- • **Choose a Body length;**
- • **Choose a Sleeve length;**
- • **Sew on the buttons or zipper and you're done!**

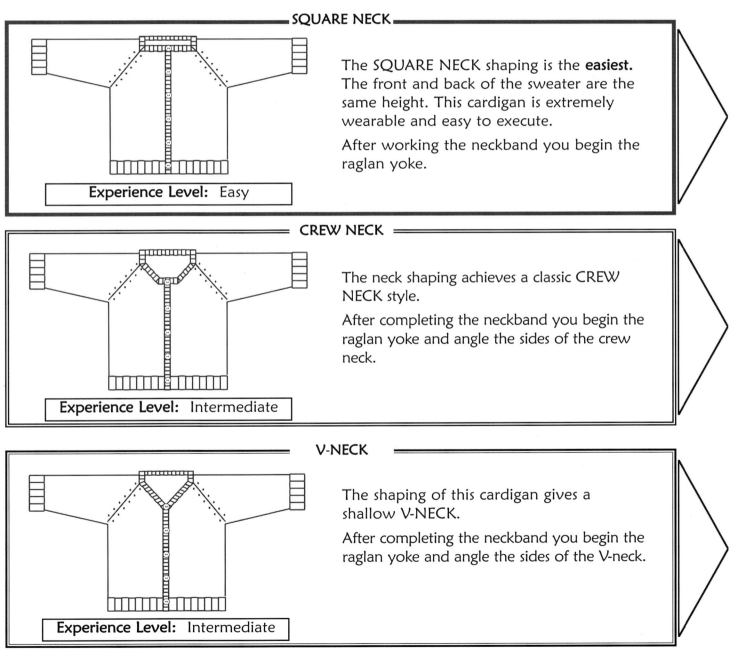

SQUARE NECK

The SQUARE NECK shaping is the **easiest.** The front and back of the sweater are the same height. This cardigan is extremely wearable and easy to execute.

After working the neckband you begin the raglan yoke.

Experience Level: Easy

CREW NECK

The neck shaping achieves a classic CREW NECK style.

After completing the neckband you begin the raglan yoke and angle the sides of the crew neck.

Experience Level: Intermediate

V-NECK

The shaping of this cardigan gives a shallow V-NECK.

After completing the neckband you begin the raglan yoke and angle the sides of the V-neck.

Experience Level: Intermediate

BASIC DK CARDIGAN

SQUARE NECK

- Basic DK Square Neck;
- Long length body; ;
- Long sleeves
- Buttonholes every 5 repeats.

| Experience Level: Easy |

Sample knit in Pumpkin Pie, Cotton Tweed DK.
Bull's Eye Buttons.

CREW NECK

- Basic DK Crew Neck;
- Hip length body;
- Short sleeves;
- Buttonholes every 3 repeats (see page 14, 24).

| Experience Level: Intermediate |

Sample knit in Purple Iris Butterfly Super 10 Cotton.
Bull's Eye Buttons.

V-NECK

- Basic DK V-Neck;
- Long length body;
- Long sleeves;
- Buttonholes every 5 repeats.

| Experience Level: Intermediate |

Sample knit in Cream, Tatamy Tweed.
Bull's Eye Buttons.

BASIC DK CARDIGAN

SQUARE NECK

BEGIN WITH THE NECKBAND

With larger circular needle, **Cast On** 98 (102, 106, 106, 106, 106) sts.

Work back and forth on circular needle:

Row 1: (RS) *With smaller circular needle,* work [K2, P2] to last 2 sts, K2.

Row 2: P2, work [K2, P2] to end of row.

Repeat last 2 rows for ¾"/2 cm.

Place first buttonhole in right buttonhole band in next row as follows:

Buttonhole Row: (RS) Work [K2, P2] to last 6 sts, K2, YO, P2tog, K2.

Last Row: *With larger circular needle,* work in rib as established increasing 2 sts evenly across row. - 100 (104, 108, 108, 108, 108) sts

CREW NECK

BEGIN WITH THE NECKBAND

With larger circular needle, **Cast On** 114 (118, 122, 122, 122, 122) sts.

Work back and forth on circular needle:

Row 1: (RS) *With smaller circular needle,* work [K2, P2] to last 2 sts, K2.

Row 2: P2, work [K2, P2] to end of row.

Repeat last 2 rows for ¾"/2 cm.

Place first buttonhole in right buttonhole band in next row as follows:

Buttonhole Row: (RS) Work [K2, P2] to last 6 sts, K2, YO, P2tog, K2.

Last Row: *With larger circular needle,* work in rib as established increasing 2 sts evenly across row. - 116 (120, 124, 124, 124, 124) sts

V-NECK

BEGIN WITH THE NECKBAND

With larger circular needle, **Cast On** 130 (138, 142, 146, 146, 150) sts.

Work back and forth on circular needle:

Row 1: (RS) *With smaller circular needle,* work [K2, P2] to last 2 sts, K2.

Row 2: P2, work [K2, P2] to end of row.

Repeat last 2 rows for ¾"/2 cm.

Place first buttonhole in right buttonhole band in next row as follows:

Buttonhole Row: (RS) Work [K2, P2] to last 6 sts, K2, YO, P2tog, K2.

Some sizes need to adjust stitch numbers for Yoke on following Last Row:

Last Row for Sizes 39 (44, 50½)"/99 (112, 128.5) cm ONLY: *With larger circular needle,* work in rib as established increasing 2 sts evenly across row. - 132 (144, 148) sts

Last Row for Sizes 42 (47, 53½)"/106.5 (119.5, 136) cm ONLY: *With larger circular needle,* work in rib as established. - 138 (146, 150) sts

Reality check: *You should have 132 (138, 144, 146, 148, 150) sts on your needle.*

Basic DK Cardigan

SQUARE NECK

SHOULDER

The Yoke is shaped by placing 4 Markers and working a pair of increases at each of these Markers every other row, giving the yoke it's distinctive raglan lines.

Note: Each of the 4 raglan Markers is set between 2 knit stitches which separate the pair of increases.

Continue to work on larger circular needle.

Set-Up Increase Row: (RS) K20 (21, 22, 23, 24, 25), INC-1, K1, Place Marker, K1, INC-1, K10 (10, 10, 8, 6, 4), INC-1, K1, Place Marker, K1, INC-1, K32 (34, 36, 38, 40, 42), INC-1, K1, Place Marker, K1, INC-1, K10 (10, 10, 8, 6, 4), INC-1, K1, Place Marker, K1, INC-1, K20 (21, 22, 23, 24, 25). - 108 (112, 116, 116, 116, 116) sts on needle.

Set-Up Straight Row: Purl.

CREW NECK

SHOULDER

The Yoke is shaped by placing 4 Markers and working a pair of increases at each of these Markers every other row, giving the yoke it's distinctive raglan lines.

Note: Each of the 4 raglan Markers is set between 2 knit stitches which separate the pair of increases.

SHORT ROW SHAPING

Short Rows are used to lower the front of the cardigan. They are so named because you only work part way across the row, then turn, leaving the rest of the sts in the row unworked on the needle. The short

rows choices for this project give a smooth angle to the side of the crew neck. Short rows are worked below:

Continue to work on larger circular needle.

Increase SHORT Row 1: (RS) K28 (29, 30, 31, 32, 33), INC-1, K1, Place Marker#1, K1, INC-1, K10 (10, 10, 8, 6, 4), INC-1, K1, Place Marker#2, K1, INC-1, K32 (34, 36, 38, 40, 42), INC-1, K1, Place Marker#3, K1, INC-1, K10 (10, 10, 8, 6, 4), INC-1, K1, Place Marker#4, K1, INC-1, *SSK, K1, TURN.*

Wrong Side SHORT Row 2: SL1, purl to Marker#1, slip Marker, P2, *P2tog, P1, TURN.*

V-NECK

SHOULDER

The Yoke is shaped by placing 4 Markers and working a pair of increases at each of these Markers every other row, giving the yoke it's distinctive raglan lines.

Note: Each of the 4 raglan Markers is set between 2 knit stitches which separate the pair of increases.

SHORT ROW SHAPING

Short Rows are used to shape the front of the cardigan. They are so named because you only work part way across the row, then turn, leaving the rest of the sts in the row unworked on the needle. The short rows chosen for this project give a smooth

angle to the side of the V-neck. Short rows are worked below:

Continue to work with the larger circular needle.

Increase SHORT Row 1: (RS) K36 (38, 40, 42, 44, 46), INC-1, K1, Place Marker#1, K1, INC-1, K10 (10, 10, 8, 6, 4), INC-1, K1, Place Marker#2, K1, INC-1, K32 (34, 36, 38, 40, 42), INC-1, K1, Place Marker#3, K1, INC-1, K10 (10, 10, 8, 6, 4), INC-1, K1, Place Marker#4, K1, INC-1, *SSK, K1, TURN.*

Wrong Side SHORT Row 2: SL1, purl to Marker#1, slip Marker, P2, *P2tog, P1, TURN.*

Basic DK Cardigan

SQUARE NECK

Skip this page and go to directly to "Common Elements"
on following page to continue Yoke.

CREW NECK

Increase SHORT Row 3: (RS) SL1, *knit to 1 stitch before Marker, INC-1, K1, slip Marker, K1, INC-1; repeat from * 3 more times, knit to 1 stitch before the gap, *SSK, K1, TURN.*

Wrong Side SHORT Row 4: SL1, purl around past Marker#1 to 1 stitch before the gap, *P2tog, P1, TURN.*

Repeat SHORT Rows 3 & 4, five more times.

Note: You should have 13 (14, 15, 16, 17, 18) sts left unworked at each end of needle.

Last Increase SHORT Row: (RS) SL1, *knit to one stitch before Marker, INC-1, K1, slip Marker, K1, INC-1; repeat from * 3 more times, knit to one stitch before the gap, *SSK, KNIT TO END OF ROW.*

Last Wrong Side SHORT Row: Purl around past Marker#1 to 1 stitch before the gap, *P2tog, PURL TO END OF ROW.*

Short Row shaping is complete!

All rows will now be worked across all sts on needle. Go to "Common Elements" on following page to continue Yoke.

V-NECK

Increase SHORT Row 3: (RS) SL1, *knit to 1 stitch before Marker, INC-1, K1, slip Marker, K1, INC-1; repeat from * 3 more times, knit to 1 stitch before the gap, *SSK, K1, TURN.*

Wrong Side SHORT Row 4: SL1, purl around past Marker#1 to 1 stitch before the gap, *P2tog, P1, TURN.*

Repeat SHORT Rows 3 & 4, 13 (14, 15, 16, 17, 18) more times.

Note: You should now have 5 sts left unworked at each end of needle.

Last Increase SHORT Row: (RS) SL1, *knit to one stitch before Marker, INC-1, K1, slip Marker, K1, INC-1; repeat from * 3 more times, knit to one stitch before the gap, *SSK, KNIT TO END OF ROW.*

Last Wrong Side SHORT Row: Purl around past Marker#1 to 1 stitch before the gap, *P2tog, PURL TO END OF ROW.*

Short Row shaping is complete!

All rows will now be worked across all sts on needle. Go to "Common Elements" on following page to continue Yoke.

Instructions below for ALL NECKLINES:

YOKE

First and last 4 sts of every row are the Front band sts.

Buttonhole Placement

Buttonholes are set approximately 3"/7.5 cm apart in instructions below.

Options:

For buttonholes placed closer together (see pg 10): The first buttonhole is in the neckband. For the second buttonhole substitute the Buttonhole Row for Row 3 the first time you *repeat* Rows 3-6 and then continue to work Buttonhole Row every 3rd repeat of Rows 3-6.

For the 2 x 2 buttonholes (see pg 20): First buttonhole is in the neckband, for second buttonhole, substitute Buttonhole Row for the first Row 3. Substitute Buttonhole Row on every following 4th and 6th repeats of Rows 3-6.

Increase Row 1: (RS) P4 (button band), *Knit to one stitch before the Marker, INC-1, K1, slip Marker, K1, INC-1; repeat from * 3 more times, knit to last 4 sts, P4 (buttonhole band).

Straight Row 2: K4 (band), purl to last 4 sts, K4 (band).

Increase Row 3: K4 (button band), *Knit to one stitch before the Marker, INC-1, K1, slip Marker, K1, INC-1; repeat from * 3 more times, knit to last 4 sts, K4 (buttonhole band).

Straight Row 4: P4 (band), purl to last 4 sts, P4 (band).

Increase Row 5: P4 (button band), *Knit to one stitch before the Marker, INC-1, K1, slip Marker, K1, INC-1; repeat from * 3 more times, knit to last 4 sts, P4 (buttonhole band).

Straight Row 6: K4 (band), purl to last 4 sts, K4 (band).

Repeat Rows 3 - 6 twice more.

In next repeat of Rows 3 - 6 place second buttonhole by substituting Buttonhole Row for Row 3 as follows:

Buttonhole Row: Substitute for Row 3: (RS) K4 (button band), *Knit to one stitch before the Marker, INC-1, K1, slip Marker, K1, INC-1; repeat from * 3 more times, knit to last 4 sts, K1, YO, K2tog, K1 (buttonhole band).

Note: Buttonhole placement is different than in the neckband.

Work Rows 4, 5, & 6 above.

Repeat Rows 3 - 6 above, until 356 (376, 396, 420, 444, 468) sts on needle, working a Buttonhole every 5th set of repeats of Rows 3 - 6.

Reality Check: Number of stitches between Markers: Both Fronts have 53 (56, 59, 63, 67, 71) sts, sleeves have 76 (80, 84, 88, 92, 96) sts, Back has 98 (104, 110, 118, 126, 134) sts.

Work 6 (6, 6, 4, 4, 4) rows even with no further increasing, continuing the Front bands as established. You may lengthen Yoke depth by working extra rows if desired. *You still have 356 (376, 396, 420, 444, 468) sts.*

Divide for Sleeves and Body: With right side facing, work 4 sts of button band as set, K49 (52, 55, 59, 63, 67) sts to first raglan Marker, remove Marker, place next 76 (80, 84, 88, 92, 96) sts of sleeve on spare yarn, remove Marker, Cast On 9 (11, 11, 11, 13, 13) sts for underarm, K98 (104, 110, 118, 126, 134) sts of Back, remove marker, place next 76 (80, 84, 88, 92, 96) sts of sleeve on spare yarn, remove Marker, Cast On 9 (11, 11, 11, 13, 13) sts for underarm, K49 (52, 55, 59, 63, 67) sts to last 4 sts, work buttonhole band as set. - 222 (238, 250, 266, 286, 302) sts on circular needle for BODY.

Next Row: Work 4 sts of band as set, purl to last 4 sts, work band as set.

BODY

Row 1: (RS) Work 4 sts of button band as set, knit to last 4 sts, work buttonhole band as set.

Row 2: Work 4 sts of band as set, purl to last 4 sts, work band as set.

Repeat last 2 rows until cardigan measures 3"/7.5 cm short of desired length (see below), ending after a Row 2.

Standard Body Lengths

Hip length - 23"/58 cm (20"/50.5 cm + 3"/7.5 cm ribbing); Cropped - 20-22"/51-56 cm (17-19"/43-48 cm for body + 3"/7.5 cm ribbing); Longer length - 27"/69 cm (24"/61 cm + 3"/7.5 cm ribbing).

CHOICE OF A TIGHT RIB OR STRAIGHT RIB (BEST FOR LONG LENGTHS):

TIGHT RIB

Row 1: (RS) Work 4 sts of button band as set, knit to last 4 sts decreasing 20 sts evenly, work buttonhole band as set.

Row 2: Work 4 sts of band as set, purl to last 4 sts, work band as set.

Row 3: *With smaller circular needle,* work 4 sts of button band as set, work [K2, P2] to last 6 sts, K2, work 4 sts in buttonhole band as set.

Row 4: Work 4 sts of band as set, P2, work [K2, P2] to last 4 sts, work band as set.

Repeat last 2 rows for 3"/7.5 cm or desired length, placing last buttonhole approximately ¾"/2 cm from bottom.

Cast Off in rib pattern.

STRAIGHT RIB

Row 1: *With smaller circular needle,* work 4 sts of button band as set, work [K2, P2]

to last 6 sts, K2, work 4 sts in buttonhole band as set.

Row 2: Work 4 sts of band as set, P2, work [K2, P2] to last 4 sts, work band as set.

Repeat last 2 rows for 3"/7.5 cm or desired length, placing last buttonhole approximately ¾"/2 cm from bottom.

Cast Off in rib pattern.

SLEEVES (WORKED IN THE ROUND): LONG, SHORT OR THREE QUARTER.

Standard Sleeve Lengths:

Long sleeve - 17"/43 cm (14"/35.5 cm + 3"/7.5 cm for the cuff); Short sleeve - 3"/7.5 cm + 1"/2.5 cm for the cuff; Three quarter sleeve - 9"/23 cm + 2"/5 cm for the cuff.

The great thing about working from the top down is you can try on your sweater and see where you like the sleeve length to be. For a man, you might add an additional 3"/7.5 cm to 8"/20 cm or even more!

LONG SLEEVES

Long Sleeve Set-Up: *With short circular needle,* starting at the centre of underarm cast on sts, attach yarn and pick up and knit 5 (6, 6, 6, 7, 7) sts from underarm cast on sts, pick up one extra st to close gap, knit around 76 (80, 84, 88, 92, 96) sleeve sts, pick up and knit one extra st to close gap, pick up and knit 4 (5, 5, 5, 6, 6) sts, join in the round and Place Marker. - 87 (93, 97, 101, 107, 111) sts

Next Round: K4 (5, 5, 5, 6, 6), K2tog, knit around sleeve sts to 5 (6, 6, 6, 7, 7) sts from end of round, SSK, knit to end of round. - 85 (91, 95, 99, 105, 109) sts

Knit 5 (5, 4, 4, 3, 3) rounds even.

Decrease Round: K1, SSK, knit to last 2 sts, K2tog.

Repeat last 6 (6, 5, 5, 4, 4) rounds until 3"/7.5 cm short of desired sleeve length. Do not decrease to less than 53 (53, 53, 57, 57, 57) sts, if necessary work straight to desired length before cuff.

CUFF

Round 1: *With double pointed needles,* knit around, decreasing evenly to 52 (52, 52, 56, 56, 56) sts.

Round 2: Work [K2, P2] to end of round.

Repeat last round for 3"/7.5 cm or desired length.

Cast Off in rib pattern.

SHORT SLEEVES

Short Sleeve Set-Up: *With short circular needle,* starting at the centre of underarm cast on sts, attach yarn and pick up and knit 5 (6, 6, 6, 7, 7) sts from underarm cast on sts, pick up one extra st to close gap, knit around 76 (80, 84, 88, 92, 96) sleeve sts, pick up and knit one extra st to close gap, pick up and knit 4 (5, 5, 5, 6, 6) sts, join in the round and Place Marker. - 87 (93, 97, 101, 107, 111) sts

Next Round: K4 (5, 5, 5, 6, 6), K2tog, knit around sleeve sts to 5 (6, 6, 6, 7, 7) sts from end of round, SSK, knit to end of round. - 85 (91, 95, 99, 105, 109) sts

Decrease Round: K1, SSK, knit to last 2 sts, K2tog.

Knit 2 rounds even.

Repeat last 3 rounds until sleeve measures 3"/7.5 cm or 1"/2.5 cm short of desired sleeve length (1"/2.5 cm cuff is worked next).

CUFF

Round 1: *With double pointed needles,* knit around, decreasing evenly so that number of stitches will be divisible by 4.

Round 2: Work [K2, P2] to end of round.

Repeat last round for 1"/2.5 cm.

Cast Off in rib pattern.

THREE QUARTER SLEEVES

Three Quarter Sleeve Set-Up: *With short circular needle,* starting at the centre of underarm cast on sts, attach yarn and pick up and knit 5 (6, 6, 6, 7, 7) sts from underarm cast on sts, pick up one extra st to close gap, knit around 76 (80, 84, 88, 92, 96) sleeve sts, pick up and knit one extra st to close gap, pick up and knit 4 (5, 5, 5, 6, 6) sts, join in the round and Place Marker. - 87 (93, 97, 101, 107, 111) sts

Next Round: K4 (5, 5, 5, 6, 6), K2tog, knit around sleeve sts to 5 (6, 6, 6, 7, 7) sts from end of round, SSK, knit to end of round. - 85 (91, 95, 99, 105, 109) sts

Knit around even for 4 (3, 3, 3, 2, 2)"/10 (7.5, 7.5, 7.5, 5, 5) cm.

Decrease Round: K1, SSK, knit to last 2 sts, K2tog.

Knit 6 rounds.

Repeat last 7 rounds until sleeve measures 9"/23 cm or 2"/5 cm short of desired sleeve length.

CUFF

Round 1: *With double pointed needles,* knit around, decreasing evenly so that number of stitches will be divisible by 4.

Round 2: Work [K2, P2] to end of round.

Repeat last round for 2"/5 cm or desired length.

Cast Off in rib pattern.

THREE BASIC ARAN CARDIGANS

INSTRUCTIONS FOR THE THREE ARAN WEIGHT BASIC CARDIGANS ARE ON THE FOLLOWING PAGES.

FOR THE THREE DK WEIGHT BASIC CARDIGANS SEE PAGES 7 - 16.

THREE BASIC ARAN CARDIGANS

This Basic Aran (heavy worsted) weight cardigan has three necklines to choose from. There is a Square Neck with no shaping; a Crew Neck with shaping; and a V-neck with shaping. Options are given on the following pages for cropped, hip or long length bodies along with three sleeve length options.

designed by Deb Gemmell

To Fit Adult Chest Size of:	35"	38"	40"	43"	46"	49"
	89 cm	97 cm	102 cm	109 cm	117 cm	124 cm
FINISHED SWEATER SIZE:	39"	42"	45"	47½"	51"	54"
	99 cm	106.5 cm	114 cm	121 cm	129.5 cm	137 cm

Materials*: Aran weight (heavy worsted) yarn - 100g ball,166m/180yds
*Note: The yarn requirements are provided for a long sleeve and hip length body. Short sleeves or three quarter sleeves will require slightly less yarn as will a cropped body. A longer body will require additional yarn.

Main Colour	6	7	7	7	8	8
Ring markers	4	4	4	4	4	4

Needles:

4.5mm/US7 circular needle (24"/60 cm long) for collar and rib bottom edge

4.5mm/US7 double pointed needles for cuffs

5.0mm/US8 circular needles in 2 lengths (30"/80 cm long for Body and 16"/40 cm long for sleeves)

Tension:

18 sts = 4"/10 cm on 5.0mm/US8 needle in stocking stitch or needle needed to obtain this tension

NOTES FOR ALL NECKLINES

Please read the following Notes prior to casting on!

1. Knit, or purl, the first stitch of every row tightly to maintain an even edge along the Front Bands.

2. A larger needle is used for the Cast On to prevent the neckband from pulling in. The neckband itself is worked with the smaller circular needle. Set up the Yoke by working the last row of the neckband with the larger circular needle.

3. The neckband, yoke and body are worked on a circular needle, working back and forth. The sleeves are worked on a circular needle in the round.

4. The first and last 4 sts of the neckband will become the Front Bands for the Cardigan. The first Buttonhole is placed in the neckband. For additional options for buttonhole placement see page 24.

5. Each Increase Row adds 8 sts to the sweater yoke.

6. Measure the sleeve length from the underarm down to the wrist.

TO BEGIN

The following pattern instructions are divided into the three neck shapings.

Choose which neck shaping you wish to have and follow the boxes with arrows across the subsequent pages.

After the neck shaping is complete, all the cardigans follow the "COMMON ELEMENTS" instructions.

- Choose a Neckline Shape;
- Follow the boxes with arrows;
- Move onto the "COMMON ELEMENTS" instructions;
- Choose a Body length;
- Choose a Sleeve length;
- Sew on the buttons or zipper and you're done!

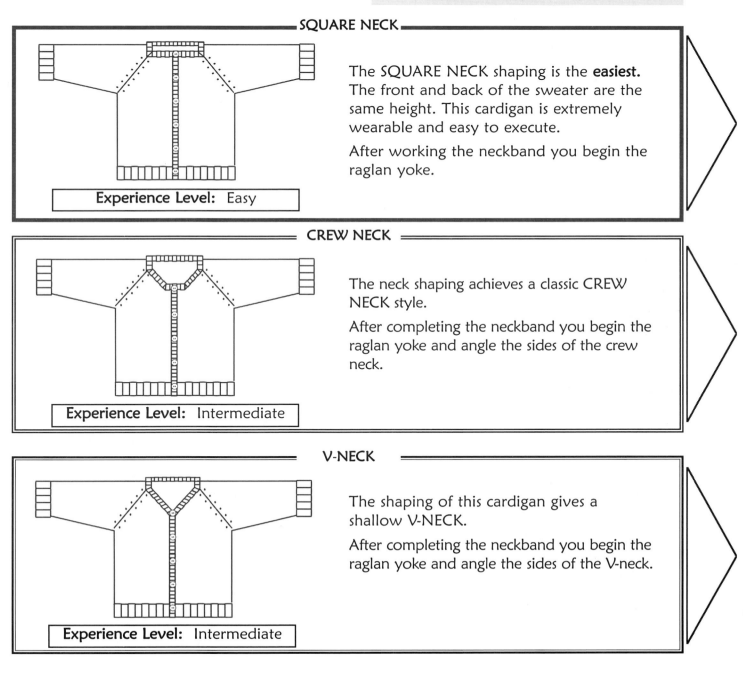

SQUARE NECK

The SQUARE NECK shaping is the **easiest**. The front and back of the sweater are the same height. This cardigan is extremely wearable and easy to execute.

After working the neckband you begin the raglan yoke.

Experience Level: Easy

CREW NECK

The neck shaping achieves a classic CREW NECK style.

After completing the neckband you begin the raglan yoke and angle the sides of the crew neck.

Experience Level: Intermediate

V-NECK

The shaping of this cardigan gives a shallow V-NECK.

After completing the neckband you begin the raglan yoke and angle the sides of the V-neck.

Experience Level: Intermediate

BASIC ARAN CARDIGAN

SQUARE NECK

- Basic Aran Square Neck;
- Hip length body;
- Long sleeves;
- Buttonholes every 5 repeats.

Experience Level: Easy

Sample knit in Sea Blue, Tatamy Tweed Worsted. Bull's Eye Buttons.

CREW NECK

- Basic Aran Crew Neck;
- Long length body;
- Long sleeves;
- Buttonholes every 5 repeats.

Experience Level: Intermediate

Sample knit in #8008, Extra Stampato Merino. Bull's Eye Buttons.

V-NECK

- Basic Aran V-Neck;
- Cropped length body;
- Three quarter length sleeves;
- 2 x 2 buttonholes (see page 24).

Experience Level: Intermediate

Sample knit in Soft Pink, CottonLicious. Bull's Eye Buttons.

BASIC ARAN CARDIGAN

SQUARE NECK

BEGIN WITH THE NECKBAND

With larger circular needle, **Cast On** 82 (86, 90, 90, 90, 90) sts.

Work back and forth on circular needle:

Row 1: (RS) *With smaller circular needle,* work [K2, P2] to last 2 sts, K2.

Row 2: P2, work [K2, P2] to end of row.

Repeat last 2 rows for ¾"/2 cm.

Place first buttonhole in right buttonhole band in next row as follows:

Buttonhole Row: (RS) Work [K2, P2] to last 6 sts, K2, YO, P2tog, K2.

Last Row: *With larger circular needle,* work in rib as established increasing 2 sts evenly across row. - 84 (88, 92, 92, 92, 92) sts

CREW NECK

BEGIN WITH THE NECKBAND

With larger circular needle, **Cast On** 94 (98, 102, 102, 102, 102) sts.

Work back and forth on circular needle:

Row 1: (RS) *With smaller circular needle,* work [K2, P2] to last 2 sts, K2.

Row 2: P2, work [K2, P2] to end of row.

Repeat last 2 rows for ¾"/2 cm.

Place first buttonhole in right buttonhole band in next row as follows:

Buttonhole Row: (RS) Work [K2, P2] to last 6 sts, K2, YO, P2tog, K2.

Last Row: *With larger circular needle,* work in rib as established increasing 2 sts evenly across row. - 96 (100, 104, 104, 104, 104) sts

V-NECK

BEGIN WITH THE NECKBAND

With larger circular needle, **Cast On** 110 (114, 122, 122, 126, 126) sts.

Work back and forth on circular needle:

Row 1: (RS) *With smaller circular needle,* work [K2, P2] to last 2 sts, K2.

Row 2: P2, work [K2, P2] to end of row.

Repeat last 2 rows for ¾"/2 cm.

Place first buttonhole in right buttonhole band in next row as follows:

Buttonhole Row: (RS) Work [K2, P2] to last 6 sts, K2, YO, P2tog, K2.

Some sizes need to adjust stitch numbers for Yoke on following Last Row:

Last Row for Sizes 42 (47½, 54)"/106.5 (121, 137) cm ONLY: *With larger circular needle,* work in rib as established increasing 2 sts evenly across row. - 116 (124, 128) sts

Last Row for Sizes 39 (45, 51)"/99 (114, 129.5) cm ONLY: *With larger circular needle,* work in rib as established. - 110 (122, 126) sts

Reality check: *You should have 110 (116, 122, 124, 126, 128) sts on your needle.*

BASIC ARAN CARDIGAN

INC-1: Increase one stitch. See pages 102 for choices of Increases.

═══ SQUARE NECK ═══

SHOULDER

The Yoke is shaped by placing 4 Markers and working a pair of increases at each of these markers every other row, giving the yoke it's distinctive raglan lines.

Note: Each of the 4 raglan Markers is set between 2 knit stitches which separate the pair of increases.

Continue to work with larger circular needle.

Set-Up Increase Row: (RS) K17 (18, 19, 20, 21, 22), INC-1, K1, Place Marker, K1, INC-1, K8 (8, 8, 6, 4, 2), INC-1, K1, Place Marker, K1, INC-1, K26 (28, 30, 32, 34, 36), INC-1, K1, Place Marker, K1, INC-1, K8 (8, 8, 6, 4, 2), INC-1, K1, Place Marker, K1, INC-1, K17 (18, 19, 20, 21, 22). - 92 (96, 100, 100, 100, 100) sts on needle

Set-Up Straight Row: Purl.

═══ CREW NECK ═══

SHOULDER

The Yoke is shaped by placing 4 Markers and working a pair of increases at each of these markers every other row, giving the yoke it's distinctive raglan lines.

Note: Each of the 4 raglan Markers is set between 2 knit stitches which separate the pair of increases.

SHORT ROW SHAPING

Short Rows are used to lower the front of the cardigan. They are so named because you only work part way across the row, then turn, leaving the rest of the sts in the row unworked on the needle. The short rows chosen for this project

give a smooth angle to the side of the crew neck. Short rows are worked below:

Continue to work with larger circular needle.

Increase SHORT Row 1: (RS) K23 (24, 25, 26, 27, 28), INC-1, K1, Place Marker#1, K1, INC-1, K8 (8, 8, 6, 4, 2), INC-1, K1, Place Marker#2, K1, INC-1, K26 (28, 30, 32, 34, 36), INC-1, K1, Place Marker#3, K1, INC-1, K8 (8, 8, 6, 4, 2), INC-1, K1, Place Marker#4, K1, INC-1, *SSK, K1, TURN.*

Wrong Side SHORT Row 2: SL1, purl to Marker#1, slip Marker, P2, *P2tog, P1, TURN.*

═══ V-NECK ═══

SHOULDER

The Yoke is shaped by placing 4 Markers and working a pair of increases at each of these markers every other row, giving the yoke it's distinctive raglan lines.

Note: Each of the 4 raglan Markers is set between 2 knit stitches which separate the pair of increases.

SHORT ROW SHAPING

Short Rows are used to shape the V-neck of the cardigan. They are so named because you only work part way across the row, then turn, leaving the rest of the sts in the row unworked on the needle.

The short rows chosen for this project give a smooth angle to the side of the V-neck. The short rows are worked below:

Continue to work with larger circular needle.

Increase SHORT Row 1: (RS) K30 (32, 34, 36, 38, 40), INC-1, K1, Place Marker#1, K1, INC-1, K8 (8, 8, 6, 4, 2), INC-1, K1, Place Marker#2, K1, INC-1, K26 (28, 30, 32, 34, 36), INC-1, K1, Place Marker#3, K1, INC-1, K8 (8, 8, 6, 4, 2), INC-1, K1, Place Marker#4, K1, INC-1, *SSK, K1, TURN.*

Wrong Side SHORT Row 2: SL1, purl to Marker#1, slip Marker, P2, *P2tog, P1, TURN.*

Basic Aran Cardigan

SQUARE NECK

Skip this page and go to directly to "Common Elements" on following page to continue Yoke.

CREW NECK

Increase SHORT Row 3: (RS) SL1, *knit to one stitch before Marker, INC-1, K1, slip Marker, K1, INC-1; repeat from * 3 more times, knit to one stitch before the gap, *SSK, K1, TURN.*

Wrong Side SHORT Row 4: SL1, purl around past Marker#1 to one stitch before the gap, *P2tog, P1, TURN.*

Repeat SHORT Rows 3 & 4, three more times.

Note: You should have 12 (13, 14, 15, 16, 17) sts left unworked on each end of needle.

Last Increase SHORT Row: (RS) SL1, *knit to one stitch before Marker, INC-1, K1, slip Marker, K1, INC-1; repeat from * 3 more times, knit to one stitch before the gap, *SSK, KNIT TO END OF ROW.*

Last Wrong Side SHORT Row: Purl around past Marker#1 to one stitch before the gap, *P2tog, PURL TO END OF ROW.*

Short Row shaping is complete!

All rows will now be worked across all sts on needle. Go to "Common Elements" on following page to continue Yoke.

V-NECK

Increase SHORT Row 3: (RS) SL1, *knit to one stitch before Marker, INC-1, K1, slip Marker, K1, INC-1; repeat from * 3 more times, knit to one stitch before the gap, *SSK, K1, TURN.*

Wrong Side SHORT Row 4: SL1, purl around past Marker#1 to one stitch before the gap, *P2tog, P1, TURN.*

Repeat SHORT Rows 3 & 4, 10 (11, 12, 13, 14, 15) more times.

Note: You should have 5 sts left unworked at each end of the needle.

Last Increase SHORT Row: (RS) SL1, *knit to one stitch before Marker, INC-1, K1, slip Marker, K1, INC-1; repeat from * 3 more times, knit to one stitch before the gap, *SSK, KNIT TO END OF ROW.*

Last Wrong Side SHORT Row: Purl around past Marker#1 to one stitch before the gap, *P2tog, PURL TO END OF ROW.*

Short Row shaping is complete!

All rows will now be worked across all sts on needle. Go to "Common Elements" on following page to continue Yoke.

Instructions below for ALL NECKLINES:

YOKE

The first and last 4 sts of every row are the Front band sts.

Buttonhole Placement

Buttonholes are set approximately 4"/10 cm apart in instructions below.

Options:

For buttonholes placed closer together (see pg 10): The first buttonhole is in the neckband. For the second buttonhole substitute the Buttonhole Row for Row 3 the first time you *repeat* Rows 3-6 and then continue to work Buttonhole Row every 3rd repeat of Rows 3-6.

For the 2 x 2 buttonholes (see pg 20): First buttonhole is in the neckband, for second buttonhole, substitute Buttonhole Row for the first Row 3. Substitute Buttonhole Row on every following 4th and 6th repeats of Rows 3-6.

Increase Row 1: P4 (button band), *Knit to one stitch before the Marker, INC-1, K1, slip Marker, K1, INC-1; repeat from * 3 more times, knit to last 4 sts, P4 (buttonhole band).

Straight Row 2: K4 (band), purl to last 4 sts, K4 (band).

Increase Row 3: K4 (button band), *Knit to one stitch before the Marker, INC-1, K1, slip Marker, K1, INC-1; repeat from * 3 more times, knit to last 4 sts, K4 (buttonhole band).

Straight Row 4: P4 (band), purl to last 4 sts, P4 (band).

Increase Row 5: P4 (button band), *Knit to 1 stitch before the Marker, INC-1, K1, slip Marker, K1, INC-1; repeat from * 3 more times, knit to last 4 sts, P4 (buttonhole band).

Straight Row 6: K4 (band), purl to last 4 sts, K4 (band).

Repeat Rows 3-6 twice more.

In next repeat of Rows 3 - 6 place the second buttonhole by working the Buttonhole Row instead of Row 3, as follows:

Buttonhole Row - substitute for Row 3: K4 (button band), *Knit to one stitch before the Marker, INC-1, K1, slip Marker, K1, INC-1; repeat from * 3 more times, knit to last 4 sts, K1, YO, K2tog, K1 (buttonhole band).

Note: Buttonhole placement is different than in the neckband.

Work Rows 4, 5, & 6 above.

Repeat Rows 3 - 6 above until 284 (304, 324, 340, 356, 372) sts on needle, working a *Buttonhole Row instead of Row 3* every 5th repeat of Rows 3 - 6.

Reality Check: Number of stitches between Markers: Both Fronts have 43 (46, 49, 52, 55, 58) sts, sleeves have 60 (64, 68, 70, 72, 74) sts, Back has 78 (84, 90, 96, 102, 108) sts.

Work 6 (6, 6, 4, 4, 4) rows even with no further increasing, continuing the Front bands as established. You may lengthen Yoke depth by working extra rows even, if desired. *You still have 284 (304, 340, 356, 372) sts.*

Divide for Sleeves and Body: With right side facing, work 4 sts of button band as set, K39 (42, 45, 48, 51, 54) sts to first raglan Marker, remove Marker, place next 60 (64, 68, 70, 72, 74) sts of sleeve on spare yarn, remove Marker, Cast On 9 (11, 11, 11, 13, 13) sts for underarm, K78 (84, 90, 96, 102, 108) sts of Back, place next 60 (64, 68, 70, 72, 74) sts of sleeve on spare yarn, remove Marker, Cast On 9 (11, 11,11, 13, 13) sts for underarm, K39 (42, 45, 48, 51, 54) sts to last 4 sts, work buttonhole band as set. - 182 (198, 210, 222, 238, 250) sts on circular needle for BODY.

Next Row: (WS) Work 4 sts of band as set, purl to last 4 sts, work band as set.

BODY

Row 1: Work 4 sts of button band as set, knit to last 4 sts, work buttonhole band as set.

Row 2: Work 4 sts of band as set, purl to last 4 sts, work band as set.

Repeat last 2 rows until cardigan measures 3"/7.5 cm short of desired length, ending after a Row 2.

Standard Body Lengths

Hip length - 23"/58 cm (20"/50.5 cm + 3"/7.5 cm ribbing); Cropped - 20-22"/51-56 cm (17-19"/43-48 cm for body + 3"/7.5 cm ribbing); Longer length - 27"/69 cm (24"/61 cm + 3"/7.5 cm ribbing).

CHOICE OF A TIGHT RIB OR STRAIGHT RIB (BEST FOR LONG LENGTHS):

BOTTOM RIB - *TIGHT*

Row 1: (RS) Work 4 sts of button band as set, knit to last 4 sts decreasing 20 sts evenly across row, work buttonhole band as set. - 162 (178, 190, 202, 218, 230) sts

Row 2: Work 4 sts of band as set, purl to last 4 sts, work band as set.

Row 3: *With smaller circular needle,* work 4 sts of button band as set, [K2, P2] to last 6 sts, K2, work 4 sts of buttonhole band as set.

Row 4: Work 4 sts of band as set, P2, [K2, P2] to last 4 sts, work band as set.

Repeat last 2 rows for 3"/7.5 cm or desired length, placing last buttonhole approximately ¾"/2 cm from bottom.

Cast Off in rib pattern.

BOTTOM RIB - *STRAIGHT*

Row 1: *With smaller circular needle,* work 4 sts of button band as set, [K2, P2] to last 6 sts, K2, work 4 sts of buttonhole band as set.

Row 2: Work 4 sts of band as set, P2, [K2, P2] to last 4 sts, work band as set.

Repeat last 2 rows for 3"/7.5 cm or desired length, placing last buttonhole approximately ¾"/2 cm from bottom.

Cast Off in rib pattern.

SLEEVES (WORKED IN THE ROUND)

You have 3 choices: LONG, SHORT OR THREE QUARTER:

Standard Sleeve Lengths

Long sleeve - 17"/43 cm (14"/35.5 cm + 3"/7.5 cm for the cuff); Short sleeve - 3"/7.5 cm + 1"/2.5 cm for the cuff; Three quarter sleeve - 9"/23 cm + 2"/5 cm for the cuff. The great thing about working from the top down is you can try on your sweater and see where you like the sleeve length to be. For a man, you might add an additional 3"/7.5 cm to 8"/20 cm or even more!

LONG SLEEVES

Long Sleeve Set-Up: *With short circular needle,* starting at the centre of underarm cast on sts, attach yarn and pick up and knit 5 (6, 6, 6, 7, 7) sts from underarm cast on sts, pick up one extra st to close gap, knit around 60 (64, 68, 70, 72, 74) sleeve sts, pick up and knit one extra st to close gap, pick up and knit 4 (5, 5, 5, 6, 6) sts, join in the round and Place Marker. - 71 (77, 81, 83, 87, 89) sts

Next Round: K4 (5, 5, 5, 6, 6), K2tog, knit around sleeve sts to 5 (6, 6, 6, 7, 7) sts from end of round, SSK, knit to end of round. - 69 (75, 79, 81, 85, 87) sts

Knit 20 (14, 8, 6, 6, 4) rounds even.

Decrease Round: K1, SSK, knit to last 2 sts, K2tog.

Knit 5 rounds even.

Sleeve Note: We've not included the numbers for the Short Sleeve and the Three Quarter cuffs as there can be a great variation in arm size. Work the decreases until your sleeve is a comfortable arm width. Continue, without decreases, if needed to achieve desired length.

Repeat last 6 rounds until 3"/7.5 cm short of desired sleeve length. Do not decrease to less than 49 (49, 49, 53, 53, 53) sts, if necessary knit even to desired sleeve length before cuff.

CUFF

Round 1: *With double pointed needles,* knit around, decreasing evenly to 44 (44, 44, 48, 48, 48) sts.

Round 2: Work [K2, P2] to end of round.

Repeat last round for 3"/7.5 cm or desired length. **Cast Off** in rib pattern.

SHORT SLEEVES

Short Sleeve Set-Up: *With short circular needle,* starting at the centre of underarm cast on sts, attach yarn and pick up and knit 5 (6, 6, 6, 7, 7) sts from underarm cast on sts, pick up one extra st to close gap, knit around 60 (64, 68, 70, 72, 74) sleeve sts, pick up and knit one extra st to close gap, pick up and knit 4 (5, 5, 5, 6, 6) sts, join in the round and Place Marker. - 71 (77, 81, 83, 87, 89) sts

Next Round: K4 (5, 5, 5, 6, 6), K2tog, knit around sleeve sts to 5 (6, 6, 6, 7, 7) sts from end of round, SSK, knit to end of round. - 69 (75, 79, 81, 85, 87) sts

Decrease Round: K1, SSK, knit to last 2 sts, K2tog.

Knit 2 rounds even.

Repeat last 3 rounds until sleeve measures 3"/7.5 cm or 1"/2.5 cm short of desired sleeve length (1"/2.5 cm cuff is worked next).

CUFF

Round 1: *With double point needles,* knit around, decreasing evenly so that number of stitches will be divisible by 4.

Round 2: Work [K2, P2] to end of round.

Repeat last round for 1"/2.5 cm. **Cast Off** in rib pattern.

THREE QUARTER LENGTH SLEEVE

Three Quarter Sleeve Set-Up: *With short circular needle,* starting at the centre of underarm cast on sts, attach yarn and pick up and knit 5 (6, 6, 6, 7, 7) sts from underarm cast on sts, pick up one extra st to close gap, knit around 60 (64, 68, 70, 72, 74) sleeve sts, pick up and knit one extra st to close gap, pick up and knit 4 (5, 5, 5, 6, 6) sts, join in the round and Place Marker. - 71 (77, 81, 83, 87, 89) sts

Next Round: K4 (5, 5, 5, 6, 6), K2tog, knit around sleeve sts to 5 (6, 6, 6, 7, 7) sts from end of round, SSK, knit to end of round. - 69 (75, 79, 81, 85, 87) sts

Knit around even for 4 (3, 3, 3, 2, 2)"/10 (7.5, 7.5, 7.5, 5, 5) cm.

Decrease Round: K1, SSK, knit to last 2 sts, K2tog.

Knit 5 rounds even.

Repeat last 6 rounds until sleeve measures 9"/23 cm or 2"/5 cm short of desired sleeve length.

CUFF

Round 1: *With double point needles,* knit around, decreasing evenly so number of stitches will be divisible by 4.

Round 2: Work [K2, P2] to end of round.

Repeat last round for 2"/5 cm or desired length.

Cast Off in rib pattern.

IDEAS FOR THE BASICS

You've now had a good look at the Basic Cardigans. Knit as they are, they make excellent sweaters. The yarn and buttons used, as you can see, make an enormous impact on the look of the finished garment. But what other variations can you make?

The following pages are all Variations on the Basic Cardigan theme by our designers. Here are some other choices you could make to the Basic Cardigans:

- yarns with interesting textures can change the whole look and season of a sweater;

- sleeve lengths can be changed;

- see the shrugs on the following pages to see what a change of yarn and a shorter body length can do!

- use a different yarn or a different colour of yarn, for the neckband and cuffs;

- stripe it;

- knit the body very long and include vents for ease of wear;

- add lace to the cuffs and bottom edging;

- make only one (large) buttonhole at the top of the sweater and use the big, bold and amazing button you have in your stash (an antique button perhaps?);

- try a zipper instead of buttons;

- work the neckband, cuffs and bottom edging in a textured stitch such as seed stitch;

- check out books like Knitting Beyond the Edge: The Essential Collection of Decorative Finishes by Nicky Epstein for all sorts of different edges.

SHRUG THOSE SHOULDERS

Little shrugs, dressy evening jackets and easy, breezy summer cover-ups are remarkably easy to achieve. On the following page you can see two examples of two quite different shrugs – both using the Basic Cardigan instructions with only minor modifications.

SOFTLY DONE

The pretty pink and orange shrug on page 30 was knit using the Aran Basic Cardigan:

- Aran (heavy worsted) Crew Neck
- three quarter length sleeves
- deep ribbing
- extra cropped body (see below)
- top buttonhole

Mom was game to see what would happen with the shrug idea using an Aran (heavy worsted) weight "thick and thin with slubs" novelty yarn.

Once she got the hang of the uneven texture (after she got a couple of inches on the needles she quite liked the look!) we decided that it would be fun to have three quarter sleeves and deep ribbing.

She worked the Aran Basic Cardigan a few inches past the underarms and then worked a long, ribbed bottom edging. Again, it was very helpful to be able to try it on as we were making decisions while she was knitting it!

You could have one buttonhole as we did or maybe three? You choose!

EVENING SPARKLES

The evening shrug on page 30 was knit using the DK Basic Cardigan:

- DK V-neck
- long sleeves
- extra cropped body (see below)
- no buttonholes.

Mom whipped up this beauty for us in a flash. She used a "rail-road" style novelty DK yarn.

She worked the DK Basic Cardigan to the underarms and then worked a short, ribbed bottom edge. She tried it on as she was working on it so it was the perfect length!

She didn't work any buttonholes and the closure options could include:

- a hook and eye closure;
- pretty ribbons to tie;
- a silver pin or clasp.

Alternatively, you could make one button-hole at the top and sew on a sparkly button!

Sample knit in #2185, SRK Mozart.
The smallest size took 10 x 50g balls.

Sample knit in colour "delight", Stylecraft Marrakech.
The smallest size took 10 x 50g balls.

SHRUG THOSE SHOULDERS

SOFTLY DONE

EVENING SPARKLES

THE VARIATIONS

COTTAGE COMFORT

An adaptation of the Basic Aran Square Neck by Deb Gemmell

Fast, easy and comfy! What more could you ask for?

- *aran weight (heavy worsted);*
- *square neck ribbed collar;*
- *long length;*
- *long sleeves;*
- *buttonholes every 6th repeat.*

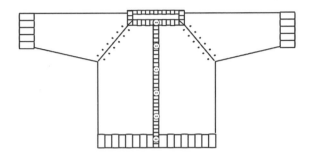

Experience Level: With Gusto!
(Enthusiastic Beginner)

To Fit Adult Chest Size of:	35" 89 cm	38" 97 cm	40" 102 cm	43" 109 cm	46" 117 cm	49" 124 cm
FINISHED SWEATER SIZE:	39" 99 cm	42" 106.5 cm	45" 114 cm	47½" 121 cm	51" 129.5 cm	54" 137 cm

Materials: Aran weight (heavy worsted) yarn - 100g ball, 168m/184yds
- 4 ring markers
- 7 or 8 buttons depending on length

Main Colour	5	6	6	7	7	8

Needles:

4.5mm/US7 circular needle (24"/60 cm long) for collar and rib bottom edge

4.5mm/US7 double pointed needles for cuffs

5.0mm/US8 circular needles in 2 lengths (30"/80 cm long for Body and 16"/40 cm long for sleeves

5.5mm/US9 circular needle (24"/60 cm long) for collar ONLY

Tension:

18 sts = 4"/10 cm on 5.0mm/US8 needle in stocking stitch or needle needed to obtain this tension.

Sample knit in Green Teal Wildridge.

Cottage Comfort

BEGIN WITH THE COLLAR

With 5.5mm/US9 circular needle, **Cast On** 82 (86, 90, 90, 90, 90) sts.

Row 1: (RS) Work [K2, P2] to last 2 sts, K2.

Row 2: P2, work [K2, P2] to end of row.

Repeat last 2 rows for 3"/7.5 cm.

Change to 4.5mm/US7 circular needle.

Repeat last 2 rows until collar measures 4½"/11.5 cm from cast on edge, ending with a wrong side row.

Work Row 1 once more.

Next Row: (WS) *With 5.0mm/US8 circular needle,* work in rib pattern as set, increasing 2 sts evenly. - 84 (88, 92, 92, 92, 92) sts

Last Row: Cast On 4 sts, purl 4 cast on sts, purl to end of row, Cast On 4 sts. - 92 (96, 100, 100, 100, 100) sts

Note: Collar is flipped over when worn so that the right side of collar is seen. The right side of the Body of the sweater is indicated below.

YOKE

The first and last 8 sts in each row are the Front bands for the cardigan. The Yoke is shaped by placing 4 Markers and working a pair of increases at each of these markers every other row, giving the yoke it's distinctive raglan lines.

Note: Each of the 4 raglan Markers is set between 2 knit sts which separate the pair of increases.

In the first row below you will place 4 raglan Markers and work the first set of increases.

Continue to work with 5.0mm/US8 circular needle.

Note: Increase used was an Open M1, page 102.

Set-Up Increase Row: (RS) K21 (22, 23, 24, 25, 26), M1, K1, Place Marker#1, K1, M1, K8 (8, 8, 6, 4, 2), M1, K1, Place Marker#2, K1, M1, K26 (28, 30, 32, 34, 36), M1, K1, Place Marker#3, K1, M1, K8 (8, 8, 6, 4, 2), M1, K1, Place Marker#4, K1, M1, K21 (22, 23, 24, 25, 26). - 100 (104, 108, 108, 108, 108) sts

Note: Each Increase Row adds 8 sts.

Set-Up Straight Row: Purl.

Increase Row 1: P8 (button band), *Knit to one st before the Marker, M1, K1, slip Marker, K1, M1; repeat from * 3 more times, knit to last 8 sts, P8 (buttonhole band).

Straight Row 2: K8 (band), purl to last 8 sts, K8 (band).

Work Rows 3 - 6 below *WITH Buttonhole, once*:

Buttonhole Row 3: K8 (button band), *Knit to one st before the Marker, M1, K1, slip Marker, K1, M1; repeat from * 3 more times, knit to last 8 sts, K3, Cast Off next 2 sts, knit to end of row (buttonhole band).

Buttonhole Row 4: P3, Cast On 2 sts, P3 (band), purl to last 8 sts, P8 (band).

Increase Row 5: P8 (button band), *Knit to one st before the Marker, M1, K1, slip Marker, K1, M1; repeat from * 3 more times, knit to last 8 sts, P8 (buttonhole band).

Straight Row 6: K8 (band), purl to last 8 sts, K8 (band).

Work Rows 3 - 6 below *WITHOUT Buttonhole, 5 Times*:

Increase Row 3: K8 (button band), *Knit to one st before the Marker, M1, K1, slip Marker, K1, M1; repeat from * 3 more times, knit to last 8 sts, K8 (buttonhole band).

Straight Row 4: P8 (band), purl to last 8 sts, P8 (band).

Increase Row 5: P8 (button band), *Knit to one st before the Marker, M1, K1, slip Marker, K1, M1; repeat from * 3 more times, knit to last 8 sts, P8 (buttonhole band).

Straight Row 6: K8 (band), purl to last 8 sts, K8 (band).

Repeat Rows 3 - 6, following the sequence above, placing a buttonhole every 6th repeat of Rows 3 - 6 until 292 (312, 332, 348, 364, 380) sts on needle

Reality Check: *Fronts have 47 (50, 53, 56, 59, 62) sts, sleeves have 60 (64, 68, 70, 72, 74) sts, Back has 78 (84, 90, 96, 102, 108) sts.*

Work 6 (6, 6, 4, 4, 4) rows even with no further increasing, continuing the Front band pattern as established. You may lengthen Yoke depth by working extra rows even, if desired. (You still have 292, 312, 332, 348, 364, 380 sts.)

Divide for Sleeves and Body: With right side facing, work 8 sts of button band as set, K39 (42, 45, 48, 51, 54) sts to first raglan Marker, remove Marker, place next 60 (64, 68, 70, 72, 74) sts of sleeve on spare yarn, remove Marker, Cast On 9 (11, 11, 11, 13, 13) sts for underarm, K78 (84, 90, 96, 102, 108) sts of Back, place next 60 (64, 68, 70, 72, 74) sts of sleeve on spare yarn, remove Marker, Cast On 9 (11, 11, 11, 13, 13) sts for underarm, K39 (42, 45, 48, 51, 54) sts to last 8 sts, work buttonhole band as set. - 190 (206, 218, 230, 246, 258) sts on circular needle for BODY.

Next Row: Work 8 sts of band as set, purl to last 8 sts, work band as set.

BODY

Row 1: Work 8 sts of button band as set, knit to last 8 sts, work buttonhole band as set.

Row 2: Work 8 sts of band as set, purl to last 8 sts, work band as set.

Repeat last 2 rows until cardigan measures 22"/56 cm or 4"/10 cm short of desired length, ending after a Row 2.

BOTTOM RIB

Row 1: *With smaller circular needle,* work 8 sts of button band as set, [K2, P2] to last 10 sts, K2, work 8 sts of buttonhole band as set.

Row 2: Work 8 sts of band as set, P2, [K2, P2] to last 8 sts, work band as set.

Repeat last 2 rows for 4"/10 cm or desired length. You may want to place one last buttonhole in the ribbing if one doesn't fall there naturally through the buttonhole row sequence.

Cast Off in rib pattern.

SLEEVES

Sleeve Set-Up: *With shorter circular needle,* starting at the centre of underarm cast on sts, attach yarn and pick up and knit 5 (6, 6, 6, 7, 7) sts from underarm cast on sts, pick up one extra st to close gap, knit around 60 (64, 68, 70, 72, 74) sleeves sts, pick up and knit one extra st to close gap, pick up and knit 4 (5, 5, 5, 6, 6, 6) sts, join in the round and Place Marker. - 71 (77, 81, 83, 87, 89) sts

Next Round: K4 (5, 5, 5, 6, 6), K2tog, knit around sleeve sts to 5 (6, 6, 6, 7, 7) sts from end of round, SSK, knit to end of round. - 69 (75, 79, 81, 85, 87) sts

Knit 20 (14, 8, 6, 6, 4) rounds even.

Decrease Round: K1, SSK, knit to last 2 sts, K2tog.

Knit 5 rounds even.

Repeat last 6 rounds until 14½"/37 cm or 2½"/6.5 cm short of desired sleeve length. Do not decrease to less than 49 (49, 49, 53, 53, 53) sts, if necessary knit straight to desired sleeve length before cuff.

DOUBLED OVER (FOLDED OVER) CUFF

Round 1: With double pointed needles, knit around, decreasing evenly to 48 (48, 48, 52, 52, 52) sts.

Round 2: Work [K2, P2] to end of round.

Repeat last round for 5"/12.5 cm or desired length.

Cast Off in rib pattern.

LakeSide Raglan

An adaptation of the Basic DK Crew Neck by Deb Gemmell

A ribbed collar transforms the Basic DK cardigan into an elegantly casual cardigan suitable for town or country.

- *DK weight;*
- *crew neck ribbed collar;*
- *hip length;*
- *long sleeves;*
- *buttonholes every 6th repeat.*

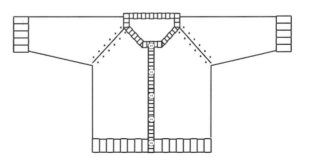

Experience Level: Intermediate

To Fit Adult Chest Size of:	35" 89 cm	38" 97 cm	40" 102 cm	43" 109 cm	46" 117 cm	49" 124 cm
FINISHED SWEATER SIZE:	39" 99 cm	42" 107 cm	44" 112 cm	47" 120 cm	50½" 12 cm	53½" 136 cm

Materials: DK yarn - 100g ball, 230m/250yds
- 4 ring markers
- 7 to 8 buttons depending on length

Main Colour	6	6	6	7	7	8

Needles:
3.25mm/US3 circular needle (24"/60 cm long) for collar and rib bottom edge
3.25mm/US3 double pointed needles for cuffs
3.75mm/US5 circular needles in 2 lengths (30"/80 cm long for Body and 16"/40 cm long for sleeves)
4.5mm/US7 circular needle (24"/60 cm long) for collar ONLY

Tension:
22 sts = 4"/10 cm on 3.75mm/US5 needle in stocking stitch or needle needed to obtain this tension.

Sample knit in Electric Blue Cotton Tweed DK. Bull's Eye Buttons.

Note: Collar, yoke and body are worked on a circular needle, working back and forth. The sleeves are worked on a circular needle in the round.

BEGIN WITH THE COLLAR

With 4.5mm/US7 needle, **Cast On** 114 (118, 122, 122, 122, 122) sts.

Row 1: (RS) Work [K2, P2] to last 2 sts, K2.

Row 2: P2, work [K2, P2] to end of row.

Repeat last 2 rows for 3"/7.5 cm.

Change to 3.25mm/US3 circular needle.

Repeat Rows 1 and 2 above until collar measures 5"/12.5 cm from cast on edge, ending with Wrong Side Row.

Last Row: (RS) *With 3.75mm/US5 circular needle,* work in rib pattern as set increasing 2 sts evenly. - 116 (120, 124, 124, 124, 124) sts

Note: Collar is flipped over when worn so that right side is seen. The right side (RS) of the sweater is indicated in instructions below.

YOKE

The Yoke is shaped by placing 4 Markers and working a pair of increases at each of these markers every other row, giving the yoke it's distinctive raglan lines.

Note: Each of the 4 raglan Markers is set between 2 knit sts which separate the pair of increases.

In the first row below you will place 4 raglan Markers, work the first set of increases and begin the SHORT Row shaping for the Crew Neck.

Continue to work with the 3.75mm/US5 circular needle (or needle needed to obtain correct tension for sweater).

Note: Each Increase Row adds 8 sts to the yoke.

Note: Increase used was an Open M1, pg 102.

SHORT ROW SHAPING for Crew Neck

Short Rows are used to lower the front of the cardigan. They are so named because you only work part way across the row, then turn, leaving the rest of the sts in the row unworked on the needle. The short rows chosen for this project give a smooth angle to the side of the crew neck. Short rows are worked below:

Increase SHORT Row 1: (RS) K28 (29, 30, 31, 32, 33), M1, K1, Place Marker#1, K1, M1, K10 (10, 10, 8, 6, 4), M1, K1, Place Marker#2, K1, M1, K32 (34, 36, 38, 40, 42), M1, K1, Place Marker#3, K1, M1, K10 (10, 10, 8, 6, 4), M1, K1, Place Marker#4, K1, M1, *SSK, K1, TURN.*

Wrong Side SHORT Row 2: SL1, purl to Marker#1, slip Marker, P2, *P2tog, P1, TURN.*

Increase SHORT Row 3: (RS) SL1, *knit to one stitch before Marker, M1, K1, slip Marker, K1, M1; repeat from * 3 more times, knit to one stitch before the gap, *SSK, K1, TURN.*

Wrong Side SHORT Row 4: SL1, purl around past Marker#1 to one stitch before the gap, *P2tog, P1, TURN.*

Repeat SHORT Rows 3 & 4, five more times.

Note: You will have 13 (14, 15, 16, 17, 18) sts left unworked at each end of needle.

Last Increase SHORT Row: (RS) SL1, *knit to one stitch before Marker, M1, K1, slip Marker, K1, M1; repeat from * 3 more times, knit to one stitch before the gap, *SSK, KNIT TO END OF ROW and Cast On 4 sts.*

Last Wrong Side SHORT Row: Purl around past Marker#1 to one stitch before the gap, *P2tog, PURL TO END OF ROW and Cast On 4 sts.*

Reality Check: You should have the following sts between markers in each section: Fronts 33 (34, 35, 36, 37, 38), Back 50 (52, 54, 56, 58, 60) sts, Sleeves 28 (28, 28, 26, 24, 22) sts.

Short Row shaping is complete! *All rows will now be worked across all sts on needle.*

CONTINUE WITH YOKE - *The first and last 8 sts of each row are Front band sts.*

Increase Row 1: (RS) P8 (button band), *Knit to one stitch before the Marker, M1, K1, slip Marker, K1, M1; repeat from * 3 more times, knit to last 8 sts, P8 (buttonhole band).

Straight Row 2: K8 (band), purl to last 8 sts, K8 (band).

Work Rows 3 - 6 below WITH Buttonhole:

Buttonhole Row (substitute for Row 3): K8 (button band), *knit to one stitch before the Marker, M1, K1, slip Marker, K1, M1; repeat from * 3 more times, knit to last 8 sts, K3, Cast Off next 2 sts, knit to end of row (buttonhole band).

Buttonhole Row (substitute for Row 4): P3, Cast On 2 sts, P3 (band), purl to last 8 sts, P8 (band).

Increase Row 5: P8 (button band), *knit to one stitch before the Marker, M1, K1, slip Marker, K1, M1; repeat from * 3 more times, knit to last 8 sts, P8 (buttonhole band).

Straight Row 6: K8 (band), purl to last 8 sts, K8.

Work Rows 3 - 6 below WITHOUT Buttonhole, 5 times:

Increase Row 3: K8 (button band), *knit to one stitch before the Marker, M1, K1, slip Marker, K1, M1; repeat from * 3 more times, knit to last 8 sts, K8 (buttonhole band).

Straight Row 4: P8 (band), purl to last 8 sts, P8 (band).

Increase Row 5: P8 (button band), *knit to one stitch before the Marker, M1, K1, slip Marker, K1, M1; repeat from * 3 more times, knit to last 8 sts, P8 (buttonhole band).

Straight Row 6: K8 (band), purl to last 8 sts, K8 (band).

Repeat Rows 3 - 6, following the sequence above, *working a Buttonhole every following 6th repeat of Rows 3-6, until 364 (384, 404, 428, 452, 476) sts on needle.*

Reality Check: Number of stitches between Markers: Both Fronts have 57 (60, 63, 67, 71, 75) sts, sleeves have 76 (80, 84, 88, 92, 96) sts, Back has 98 (104, 110, 118, 126, 134) sts.

Work 6 (6, 6, 4, 4, 4) rows even with no further increasing, *continuing the Front bands as established. You may lengthen Yoke depth by working extra rows even, if desired.* (You still have 364 (384, 404, 428, 452, 476) sts on needle.)

Divide for Sleeves and Body: With right side facing, work 8 sts of button band as set, K49 (52, 55, 59, 63, 67) sts to first raglan Marker, remove Marker, place next 76 (80, 84, 88, 92, 96) sts of sleeve on spare yarn, remove Marker, Cast On 9 (11, 11, 11, 13, 13) sts for underarm, K98 (104, 110, 118, 126, 134) sts of Back, place next 76 (80, 84, 88, 92, 96) sts of sleeve on spare yarn, remove Marker, Cast On 9 (11, 11, 11, 13, 13) sts for underarm, K49 (52, 55, 59, 63, 67) sts to last 8 sts, work buttonhole band as set. - 230 (246, 258, 274, 294, 310) sts on circular needle for BODY.

Next Row: (WS) Work 8 sts of band as set, purl to last 8 sts, work band as set.

BODY

Row 1: (RS) Work 8 sts of button band as set, knit to last 8 sts, work buttonhole band as set.

Row 2: Work 8 sts of band as set, purl to last 8 sts, work band as set.

Repeat last 2 rows until cardigan measures 19"/48 cm or 4"/10 cm short of desired length, ending after a Row 2.

BOTTOM RIB

Row 1: (RS) *With smaller circular needle,* work 8 sts of button band as set, work [K2, P2] to last 10 sts, K2, work 8 sts of buttonhole band as set.

Row 2: Work 8 sts of band as set, P2, [K2, P2] to last 8 sts, work band as set.

Repeat last 2 rows for 4"/10 cm or desired length, ending with a Right Side Row. You may want to place one last buttonhole in the ribbing if one doesn't fall there naturally through the buttonhole row sequence.

Cast Off in ribbing pattern with wrong side facing.

SLEEVES

Sleeve Set-Up: *With shorter circular needle,* starting at the centre of underarm cast on sts, attach yarn and pick up and knit 5 (6, 6, 6, 7, 7) sts from underarm cast on sts, pick up one extra st to close gap, knit around 76 (80, 84, 88, 92, 96) sleeves sts, pick up and knit one extra st to close gap, pick up and knit 4 (5, 5, 5, 6, 6) sts, join in the round and Place Marker. - 87 (93, 97, 101, 107, 111) sts

Next Round: K4 (5, 5, 5, 6, 6), K2tog, knit around sleeve sts to 5 (6, 6, 6, 7, 7) sts from end of round, SSK, knit to end of round. - 85 (91, 95, 99, 105, 109) sts

Knit 10 (10, 10, 8, 8, 8) rounds even.

Decrease Round: K1, SSK, knit to last 2 sts, K2tog.

Knit 5 rounds even.

Repeat last 6 rounds until 3"/7.5 cm short of desired sleeve length (3"/7.5 cm cuff is worked next). Do not decrease to less than 53 (53, 53, 57, 57, 57) sts, if necessary work straight to desired length before cuff.

CUFF

Round 1: *With smaller double pointed needles,* knit around, decreasing evenly to 52 (52, 52, 56, 56, 56) sts.

Round 2: Work [K2, P2] to end of round.

Repeat last round for 3"/7.5 cm.

Cast Off in rib pattern.

THE CASUAL CLASSIC

An adaption of the Basic Aran V-Neck by Deb Gemmell

Add a ribbed collar to the Basic Aran cardigan for a tailored look on this casual classic.

- *aran weight (heavy worsted);*
- *V-neck ribbed collar;*
- *cropped length;*
- *long sleeves;*
- *buttonholes every 6th repeat.*

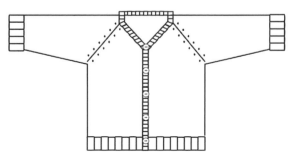

Experience Level: Intermediate

To Fit Adult Chest Size of:	35" 89 cm	38" 97 cm	40" 102 cm	43" 109 cm	46" 117 cm	49" 124 cm
FINISHED SWEATER SIZE:	39" 99 cm	42" 107 cm	45" 114 cm	47½" 121 cm	51" 130 cm	54" 137 cm

Materials: Aran weight (heavy worsted) wool - 100g ball, 268m/184yds
- 4 ring markers
- 4 or 5 buttons depending on size or length

Main Colour	5	6	6	7	7	8

Needles:
4.5mm/US7 circular needle (24"/60 cm long) for collar and rib bottom edge
4.5mm/US7 double pointed needles for cuffs
5.0mm/US8 circular needles in 2 lengths (30"/80 cm long for Body and 16"/40 cm long for sleeves)
5.5mm/US9 circular needle (24"/60 cm long) for collar ONLY

Tension:
18 sts = 4"/10 cm on 5.0mm/US8 needle in stocking stitch or needle needed to obtain this tension.

Sample knit in Beach Ball (#1306), Naturally Nazareth. Bull's Eye Buttons.

Note: *Neckband, yoke and body are worked on a circular needle, working back and forth. The sleeves are worked on a circular needle in the round.*

BEGIN WITH THE COLLAR

With 5.5mm/US9 circular needle, **Cast On** 110 (114, 122, 122, 126, 126) sts.

Row 1: (RS) Work [K2, P2] to last 2 sts, K2.

Row 2: P2, work [K2, P2] to end of row.

Repeat last 2 rows for 3"/7.5 cm.

Change to 4.5mm/US7 circular needle.

Repeat last 2 rows until collar measures 5"/12.5 cm from cast on edge, ending with a wrong side row.

Some sizes need to adjust stitch numbers for Yoke:

Sizes 42 (47½, 54)"/107 (121, 137) cm ONLY

Last Row: (RS) *With 5.0mm/US8 circular needle,* work in rib pattern as set, increasing 2 sts evenly. - 116 (124, 128) sts

Sizes 39 (45, 51)"/99 (114, 130) cm ONLY:

Last Row: (RS) *With 5.0mm/US8 circular needle,* work in rib pattern as set. - 110 (122, 126) sts

Reality Check: *You should now have 110 (116, 122, 124, 126, 128) sts.*

The collar will be flipped over when worn so that the right side rows are seen. The right side (RS) for the sweater is indicated in the instructions below.

YOKE

The Yoke is shaped by working a pair of increases at each of the 4 markers every other row, giving the yoke it's distinctive raglan lines.

In the first row below you will place 4 raglan Markers and work the first set of increases.

Note: *Each of the 4 raglan Markers is set between 2 knit sts which separate the pair of increases.*

SHORT ROW SHAPING for V-Neck

Short Rows are used to shape the V-neck of the cardigan. They are so named because you only work part way across the row, then turn, leaving the rest of the sts in the row unworked on the needle. The short rows chosen for this project give a smooth angle to the side of the V-neck. The short rows are worked below:

Continue to work with middle sized circular needle needed to obtain correct tension for the sweater.

Increase SHORT Row 1: (RS) K30 (32, 34, 36, 38, 40), M1, K1, Place Marker#1, K1, M1, K8 (8, 8, 6, 4, 2), M1, K1, Place Marker#2, K1, M1, K26 (28, 30, 32, 34, 36), M1, K1, Place Marker#3, K1, M1, K8 (8, 8, 6, 4, 2), M1, K1, Place Marker#4, K1, M1, *SSK, K1, TURN.*

Note: *Each Increase Row adds 8 sts to the sweater yoke.*

Wrong Side SHORT Row 2: SL1, purl to Marker#1, slip Marker, P2, *P2tog, P1, TURN.*

Increase SHORT Row 3: (RS) SL1, *knit to one stitch before Marker, M1, K1, slip Marker, K1, M1; repeat from * 3 more times, knit to *one stitch before the gap, SSK, K1, TURN.*

Wrong Side SHORT Row 4: SL1, purl around past Marker#1 to *one stitch before the gap,* P2tog, P1, TURN.

Repeat SHORT Rows 3 & 4, 10 (11, 12, 13, 14, 15) more times.

Note: *You should have 5 sts left unworked on each end of needle.*

Last Increase SHORT Row: (RS) SL1, *knit to one stitch before Marker, M1, K1, slip Marker, K1, M1; repeat from * 3 more times, knit to *one stitch before the gap, SSK, KNIT TO END OF ROW and Cast On 4 sts.*

Last Wrong Side SHORT Row: Purl around past Marker#1 to *one stitch before the gap, P2tog, PURL TO END OF ROW and Cast On 4 sts.*

Short Row shaping is complete! All rows will now be worked across all sts on needle.

CONTINUE WITH YOKE:

The first and last 8 sts on your needle are for the Front bands.

Increase Row 1: (RS) P8 (button band), *Knit to one stitch before the Marker, M1, K1, slip Marker, K1, M1; repeat from * 3 more times, knit to last 8 sts, P8 (buttonhole band).

Straight Row 2: K8 (band), purl to last 8 sts, K8 (band).

Work Rows 3 - 6 below WITH Buttonhole, once:

Buttonhole Row (substitute for Row 3): K8 (button band), *Knit to one stitch before the Marker, M1, K1, slip Marker, K1, M1; repeat from * 3 more times, knit to last 8 sts, K3, Cast Off next 2 sts, knit to end of row (buttonhole band).

Buttonhole Row (substitute for Row 4): P3, Cast On 2 sts, P3 (band), Purl to last 8 sts, P8 (band).

Increase Row 5: P8 (button band), *Knit to one stitch before the Marker, M1, K1, slip Marker, K1, M1; repeat from * 3 more times, knit to last 8 sts, P8 (buttonhole band).

Straight Row 6: K8 (band), purl to last 8 sts, K8 (band).

Work Rows 3 - 6 below WITHOUT Buttonhole, 5 Times:

Increase Row 3: K8 (button band), *Knit to one stitch before the Marker, M1, K1, slip Marker, K1, M1; repeat from * 3 more times, knit to last 8 sts, K8 (buttonhole band).

Straight Row 4: P8 (band), purl to last 8 sts, P8 (band).

Increase Row 5: P8 (button band), *Knit to one stitch before the Marker, M1, K1, slip Marker, K1, M1; repeat from * 3 more times, knit to last 8 sts, P8 (buttonhole band).

Straight Row 6: K8 (band), purl to last 8 sts, K8 (band).

Repeat Rows 3 - 6, following the sequence above, working a buttonhole every 6th repeat of Rows 3 - 6 until 292 (312, 332, 348, 364, 380) sts on needle.

Reality Check: *Number of stitches between Markers: Both Fronts have 47 (50, 53, 56, 59, 62) sts, sleeves have 60 (64, 68, 70, 72, 74) sts, Back has 78 (84, 90, 96, 102, 108) sts.*

Work 6 (6, 6, 4, 4, 4) rows even with no further increasing, continuing the Front bands as established. You may lengthen Yoke depth by working extra rows even, if desired. (You still have 292, 312, 332, 348, 364, 380 sts.)

Divide for Sleeves and Body: With right side facing, work 8 sts of button band as set, K39 (42, 45, 48, 51, 54) sts to first raglan Marker, remove Marker, place next 60 (64, 68, 70, 72, 74) sts of sleeve on spare yarn, remove Marker, Cast On 9 (11, 11, 11, 13, 13) sts for underarm, K78 (84, 90, 96, 102, 108) sts of Back, place next 60

THE CASUAL CLASSIC

(64, 68, 70, 72, 74) sts of sleeve on spare yarn, remove Marker, Cast On 9 (11, 11, 11, 13, 13) sts for underarm, K39 (42, 45, 48, 51, 54) sts to last 8 sts, work buttonhole band as set. - 190 (206, 218, 230, 246, 258) sts on circular needle for BODY.

Next Row: Work 8 sts of band as set, purl to last 8 sts, work band as set.

BODY

Row 1: Work 8 sts of button band as set, knit to last 8 sts, work buttonhole band as set.

Row 2: Work 8 sts of band as set, purl to last 8 sts, work band as set.

Repeat last 2 rows until cardigan measures 2"/5 cm short of desired length, ending after a Row 2.

BOTTOM RIB

Row 1: *With smaller circular needle*, work 8 sts of button band as set, [K2, P2] to last 10 sts, K2, work 8 sts of buttonhole band as set.

Row 2: Work 8 sts of band as set, P2, [K2, P2] to last 8 sts, work band as set.

Repeat last 2 rows for 2"/5 cm or desired length, ending with right side row. Place one last buttonhole in the ribbing if one doesn't fall there naturally through the buttonhole row sequence.

Cast Off in rib pattern.

SLEEVES

Sleeve Set-Up: *With shorter circular needle*, starting at the centre of underarm sts, attach yarn and pick up and knit 5 (6, 6, 6, 7, 7) sts from underarm cast on sts , pick up one extra st to close gap, knit around 60 (64, 68, 70, 72, 74) sleeves sts, pick up and knit one extra st to close gap, pick up and knit 4 (5, 5, 5, 6, 6, 6) sts, join in the round and Place Marker. - 71 (77, 81, 83, 87, 89) sts

Next Round: K4 (5, 5, 5, 6, 6), K2tog, knit around sleeve sts to 5 (6, 6, 6, 7, 7) sts from end of round, SSK, knit to end of round. - 69 (75, 79, 81, 85, 87) sts

Knit 20 (14, 8, 6, 6, 4) rounds even.

Decrease Round: K1, SSK, knit to last 2 sts, K2tog.

Knit 5 rounds even.

Repeat last 6 rounds until 2"/5 cm short of desired sleeve length. Do not decrease to less than 45 (45, 45, 49, 49, 49) sts.

CUFF

Round 1: With double pointed needles, knit around, decreasing evenly to 44 (44, 44, 48, 48, 48) sts.

Round 2: Work [K2, P2] to end of round.

Repeat last round for 2"/5 cm or desired length.

Cast Off in rib pattern.

SUMMER-TIME TOP

An adaptation of the Basic DK Square Neck by Deb Gemmell

Lively striping adds sparkle to this classic summer top. Team with The Basic DK Crew-Neck for a terrific, and easy, twin set.

- *DK weight;*
- *square neck;*
- *cropped length;*
- *short sleeves;*
- *picked up button band.*

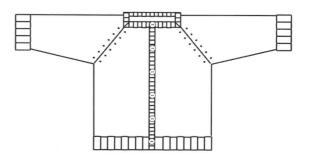

Experience Level: With Gusto!
(Enthusiastic Beginner)

To Fit Adult Chest Size of:	35" 89 cm	38" 97 cm	40" 102 cm	43" 109 cm	46" 117 cm	49" 124 cm
FINISHED SWEATER SIZE:	39" 99 cm	42" 106.5 cm	44" 112 cm	47" 119.5 cm	50½" 128.5 cm	53½" 136 cm

Materials: DK yarn - 100g ball, 230m/250yds
- 4 ring markers
- the number of buttons depends on the stitches picked up along Front Bands.

Main Colour	2	2	2	2	2	2
Contrast Colour 1	2	2	2	2	2	2
Contrast Colour 2	2	2	2	2	2	2

Needles:

3.25mm/US3 circular needle (24"/60 cm long) for neckband and ribbed bottom edge

3.25mm/US3 double pointed needles for cuffs - optional

3.75mm/US5 circular needles in 2 lengths (30"/80 cm long for Body and 16"/40 cm long for sleeves).

Tension:

22 sts = 4"/10 cm on 3.75mm/US5 needle in stocking stitch or needle needed to obtain this tension.

Sample knit in Denim, Pumpkin Pie and Cream, Cotton Tweed DK. Bull's Eye Buttons.

Note: Neckband, yoke and body are worked on a circular needle, working back and forth. The sleeves are worked on a circular needle in the round.

BEGIN WITH THE NECKBAND

With smaller circular needle and Main Colour, **Cast On** 122 (126, 130, 130, 130, 130) sts.

Row 1: (RS) Work [K2, P2] to last 2 sts, K2.

Row 2: P2, work [K2, P2] to end of row.

Repeat last 2 rows for ½"/1.5 cm.

Work Row 1 once more.

Last Row: *With larger circular needle,* work in rib as established, increasing 2 sts evenly across row. - 124 (128, 132, 132, 132, 132) sts

YOKE

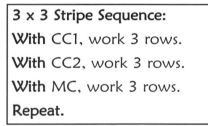

> **3 x 3 Stripe Sequence:**
> With CC1, work 3 rows.
> With CC2, work 3 rows.
> With MC, work 3 rows.
> **Repeat.**

The Yoke is shaped by placing 4 Markers and working a pair of increases at each of these Markers every other row, giving the yoke it's distinctive raglan lines.

Note: Each of the 4 raglan Markers is set between 2 knit sts which separate the pair of increases.

In the first row below you will place 4 raglan Markers and work the first set of increases.

Note: Increase used was a Open M1, page 102.
Continue to work on larger circular needle.

Work the following rows of Yoke and Body in 3x3 Stripes Sequence as above.

Set-Up Increase Row: (RS) With Contrast Colour 1 (CC1), K20 (21, 22, 23, 24, 25), M1, K1, Place Marker, K1, M1, K18 (18, 18, 16, 14, 12), M1, K1, Place Marker, K1, M1, K40 (42, 44, 46, 48, 50), M1, K1, Place Marker, K1, M1, K18 (18, 18, 16, 14, 12), M1, K1, Place Marker, K1, M1, K20 (21, 22, 23, 24, 25). - 132 (136, 140, 140, 140, 140) sts

Note: Each Increase Row adds 8 sts to the sweater yoke.

Straight Row: Purl.

Increase Row: *Knit to one stitch before the Marker, M1, K1, slip Marker, K1, M1; repeat from * 3 more times, knit to end of row.

Straight Row: With CC2, Purl.

Increase Row: *Knit to one stitch before the Marker, M1, K1, slip Marker, K1, M1; repeat from * 3 more times, knit to end of row.

Straight Row: Purl.

Increase Row: With MC, *Knit to one stitch before the Marker, M1, K1, slip Marker, K1, M1; repeat from * 3 more times, knit to end of row.

Straight Row: Purl.

Increase Row: *Knit to one stitch before the Marker, M1, K1, slip Marker, K1, M1; repeat from * 3 more times, knit to end of row.

Straight Row: With CC1, Purl.

Continue repeating the Increase and Straight Rows in 3x3 Stripe Sequence, until 348 (368, 388, 412, 436, 460) sts on needle.

Reality Check: Number of stitches between Markers: Both Fronts have 49 (52, 55, 59, 63, 67) sts, sleeves have 76 (80, 84, 88, 92, 96) sts, Back has 98 (104, 110, 118, 126, 134) sts.

Summer-Time Top sample knit in Denim, Pumpkin Pie and Cream, Cotton Tweed DK. The Basic DK Square-Neck Cardigan was knit in Pumpkin Pie, Cotton Tweed DK.

Work 6 (6, 6, 4, 4, 4) rows even with no further increasing. You may lengthen Yoke depth by working extra rows if desired. (You still have 348, 368, 388, 412, 436, 460 sts.)

Divide for Sleeves and Body: With right side facing, K49 (52, 55, 59, 63, 67) sts to first raglan Marker, remove Marker, place next 76 (80, 84, 88, 92, 96) sts of sleeve on spare yarn, remove Marker, Cast On 9 (11, 11, 11, 13, 13) sts for underarm, K98 (104, 110, 118, 126, 134) sts of Back, place next 76 (80, 84, 88, 92, 96) sts of sleeve on spare yarn, remove Marker, Cast On 9 (11, 11, 11, 13, 13) sts for underarm, K49 (52, 55, 59, 63, 67) sts. - 214 (230, 242, 258, 278, 294) sts on circular needle for BODY

Next Row: Purl.

BODY

Row 1: (RS) Knit.

Row 2: Purl.

Repeat last 2 rows, continuing in 3x3 Stripes Sequence until cardigan measures 1"/2.5 cm short of desired length, ending with a completed CC2 stripe (approximately 18"/45.5 cm to 21"/53 cm long - your choice.

Note: Your last row of the CC2 stripe may be either a right side or a wrong side row. This is correct.

BOTTOM RIB

Set-Up Row: With MC, work first row in stockinette stitch (knit or purl, whichever is appropriate).

Sample knit in Marble, allhemp6.

With smaller circular needle, begin with the appropriate row below depending on whether the right side or wrong side of work is facing you:

Right Side Row: Work [K2, P2] to last 2 sts, K2.

Wrong Side Row: P2, work [K2, P2].

Continue to work last 2 rows for 1"/2.5 cm or desired length, ending after a Right Side Row.

With Wrong Side facing, **Cast Off** in ribbing pattern.

SLEEVES (WORKED IN THE ROUND)

Sleeve Set-Up: *With shorter circular needle,* starting at the centre of underarm cast on sts, attach yarn in appropriate colour to continue in 3x3 Stripe Sequence for sleeve and pick up and knit 5 (6, 6, 6, 7, 7) sts from underarm cast on sts, pick up one extra st to close gap, knit around 76 (80, 84, 88, 92, 96) sleeves sts, pick up and knit one extra st to close gap, pick up and knit 4 (5, 5, 5, 6, 6) sts, join in the round and Place Marker. - 87 (93, 97, 101, 107, 111) sts

Continue to work sleeve in 3x3 Stripe Sequence.

Next Round: K4 (5, 5, 5, 6, 6), K2tog, knit around sleeve sts to 5 (6, 6, 6, 7, 7) sts from end of round, SSK, knit to end of round. - 85 (91, 95, 99, 105, 109) sts

Knit number of rounds needed (0, 1 or 2 rounds) to finish the stripe you are working on.

In Next Stripe:

Decrease Round: K1, SSK, knit to last 2 sts, K2tog.

Knit 2 rounds even.

Repeat last 3 rounds in 3x3 Stripe Sequence until sleeve measures approximately 2"/5 cm or ½"/1.5 cm short of desired sleeve length (½"/1.5 cm cuff to be worked next). End after completing a CC2 stripe for Main Colour Cuff.

CUFF

Round 1: Continue with smaller double pointed needles and Main Colour, knit around, decreasing evenly so that number of stitches will be divisible by 4.

Round 2: Work [K2, P2] to end of round.

Repeat last round for ½"/1.5 cm or desired length of cuff.

Cast Off in rib pattern.

FRONT BANDS

Left Button band: With right side facing, using smaller circular needle and Main Colour, starting at the top of the Left Front, pick up and knit 2 sts in the *first stripe* and every following stripe down the Front, pick up either 4 or 6 sts along the side of the bottom ribbing whichever number of stitches will make the total number of band sts divisible by 4 to fit the rib pattern.

Working back and forth on circular needle:

Next Row: Work [K2, P2] to end of row.

Repeat last row 3 times more, ending after right side row.

Cast Off in rib with wrong side facing.

Right Buttonhole band: With right side facing using smaller circular needle and Main Colour, starting at the bottom of the Right Front, pick up and knit 4 or 6 sts along the side of the bottom ribbing to match the other band, pick up and knit 2 sts for each stripe.

Working back and forth on circular needle:

Next Row: P2, work [K2, P2] to last 2 sts, K2.

Repeat last row once.

Buttonhole Row: With wrong side facing, P2, work buttonhole *[YO, K2tog], P2, K2, P2; repeat from * to the bottom of the band, ending with K2.

Note: You may look at where the buttonholes will fall and decide to place them differently in order to have the last buttonhole fall where you would like.

Next Row: (RS) Work rib as set.

Cast Off in rib with wrong side facing.

Nordic Snowflake

An adaption of the Basic Aran Crew Neck by Megan Lacey

Geometric snowflakes give an interesting twist to the simple contrast of dark and light with this winter favourite.

- *Aran (heavy worsted) weight;*
- *crew neck;*
- *hip length;*
- *buttons every 5th repeat.*

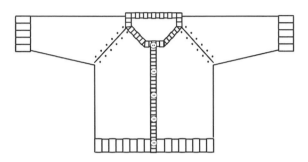

Experience Level: Intermediate

To Fit Adult Chest Size of:	35" 89 cm	38" 97 cm	40" 102 cm	43" 109 cm	46" 117 cm	49" 124 cm
FINISHED SWEATER SIZE:	39" 99 cm	42" 107 cm	45" 114 cm	47½" 121 cm	51" 130 cm	54" 137 cm

Materials: Aran weight (heavy worsted) yarn - 4 oz ball, 201 m/220 yds
- 4 ring markers
- 8 pewter buttons

Main Colour (Red)	3	4	4	5	5	6
CC1 (Navy)	2	3	3	4	4	5

Needles:

4.5mm/US7 circular needle (24"/60 cm long) for collar and ribbed bottom edge

4.5mm/US7 double pointed needles for cuffs

5.0mm/US8 circular needles in 2 lengths (30"/80 cm long for Body and 16"/40 cm long for sleeves)

Tension:

18 sts = 4"/10 cm on 5.0mm/US8 needle in stocking stitch or needle needed to obtain this tension.

Sample knit in Haw (red) and Navy, Black Water Abbey 2 ply.

Note: Neckband, yoke and body are worked on a circular needle, working back and forth. The sleeves are worked on a circular needle in the round.

BEGIN WITH THE NECKBAND

The first and last 4 sts of the Neckband will become the Front bands for the Cardigan.

Note: The neckband is Cast On with a larger circular needle to prevent the neckband from pulling in. Work the neckband itself with a smaller circular needle. Set up the Yoke by working the last row of the neckband with the larger circular needle.

With larger circular needle and CC1, **Cast On** 94 (98, 102, 102, 102, 102) sts.

Row 1: (RS) *With smaller circular needle,* work [K2, P2] to last 2 sts, K2.

Row 2: P2, work [K2, P2] to end of row.

Repeat last 2 rows for ¾"/2 cm.

Place first buttonhole in right buttonhole band in next row as follows:

Buttonhole Row: (RS) Work [K2, P2] to last 6 sts, K2, YO, P2tog, K2.

Last Row: (WS) *With larger circular needle,* work rib as set, increasing 2 sts evenly around. - 96 (100, 104, 104, 104, 104) sts

YOKE

The Yoke is shaped by placing 4 Markers and working a pair of increases at each of these markers every other row, giving the yoke it's distinctive raglan lines.

Each of the 4 raglan Markers is set between 2 knit sts which separate the pair of increases.

In the first row below you will place 4 raglan Markers, work the first set of increases and begin the SHORT Row shaping for the Crew Neck.

Please Note: *Each Increase Row adds 8 sts to the sweater yoke.*

SHORT ROW SHAPING for Crew Neck

Short Rows are used to lower the front of the cardigan. They are so named because you only work part way across the row, then turn, leaving the rest of the sts in the row unworked on the needle. The short rows chosen for this project give a smooth angle to the side of the crew neck.

Short rows are worked below.

Continue to work with larger circular needle.

Increase SHORT Row 1: (RS) K23 (24, 25, 26, 27, 28), M1, K1, Place Marker#1, K1, M1, K8 (8, 8, 6, 4, 2), M1, K1, Place Marker#2, K1, M1, K26 (28, 30, 32, 34, 36), M1, K1, Place Marker#3, K1, M1, K8 (8, 8, 6, 4, 2), M1, K1, Place Marker#4, K1, M1, *SSK, K1, TURN.*

Wrong Side SHORT Row 2: SL1, purl to Marker#1, slip Marker, P2, *P2tog, P1, TURN.*

Increase SHORT Row 3: (RS) SL1, *knit to one stitch before Marker, M1, K1, slip Marker, K1, M1; repeat from * 3 more times, knit to one stitch before the gap, *SSK, K1, TURN.*

Wrong Side SHORT Row 4: SL1, purl around past Marker#1 to one stitch before the gap, *P2tog, P1, TURN.*

Repeat SHORT Rows 3 & 4, three more times.

Last Increase SHORT Row: (RS) SL1, *knit to one stitch before Marker, M1, K1, slip Marker, K1, M1; repeat from * 3 more times, *knit to one stitch before the gap, SSK, KNIT TO END OF ROW.*

Last Wrong Side SHORT Row: Purl around past Marker#1 to *one stitch before the gap, P2tog, PURL TO END OF ROW.*

Short Row shaping is complete!

All rows will now be worked across all sts on needle.

Nordic Snowflake

Continue with YOKE: *The first and last 4 sts of every row are the Front band sts.*

Increase Row 1: (RS) P4 (button band), *Knit to one stitch before the Marker, M1, K1, slip Marker, K1, M1; repeat from * 3 more times, knit to last 4 sts, P4 (button-hole band).

Straight Row 2: K4 (band), purl to last 4 sts, K4 (band).

Increase Row 3: K4 (button band), *Knit to one stitch before the Marker, M1, K1, slip Marker, K1, M1; repeat from * 3 more times, knit to last 4 sts, K4 (buttonhole band).

Straight Row 4: P4 (band), purl to last 4 sts, P4 (band).

Increase Row 5: P4 (button band), *Knit to one stitch before the Marker, M1, K1, slip Marker, K1, M1; repeat from * 3 more times, knit to last 4 sts, P4 (buttonhole band).

Straight Row 6: K4 (band), purl to last 4 sts, K4 (band).

In the next repeat of Rows 3-6 place the second buttonhole by working the Buttonhole Row instead of Row 3 as follows:

Buttonhole Row - Substitute for Row 3: K4, (Button band), *Knit to one stitch before the Marker, M1, K1, slip Marker, K1, M1; repeat from * 3 more times, knit to last 4 sts, K1, YO, K2tog, K1 (buttonhole band).

Note: Buttonhole placement is different than in the neckband.

Repeat Rows 3-6 above until 284 (304, 324, 340, 356, 372) sts on needle, working a Buttonhole Row instead of Row 3 every 5th repeat of Rows 3-6.

Reality Check: Number of stitches between Markers: Both Fronts have 43 (46, 49, 52, 55, 58) sts, sleeves have 60 (64, 68, 70, 72, 74) sts, Back has 78 (84, 90, 96, 102, 108) sts.

Work 6 (6, 6, 4, 4, 4) rows even with no further increasing, *continuing the Front bands* as established. You may lengthen Yoke depth by working extra rows even, if desired. (You still have 284, 304, 324, 340, 356, 372 sts.)

Divide for Sleeves and Body: With right side facing, work 4 sts of button band as set, K39 (42, 45, 48, 51, 54) sts to first raglan Marker, remove Marker, place next 60 (64, 68, 70, 72, 74) sts of sleeve on spare yarn, remove Marker, Cast On 9 (11, 11, 11, 13, 13) sts for underarm, K78 (84, 90, 96, 102, 108) sts of Back, place next 60 (64, 68, 70, 72, 74) sts of sleeve on spare yarn, remove Marker, Cast On 9 (11, 11, 11, 13, 13) sts for underarm, K39 (42, 45, 48, 51, 54) sts to last 4 sts, work button band as set. - 182 (198, 210, 222, 238, 250) sts on circular needle for BODY)

Next Row: Work 4 sts of band as set, purl to last 4 sts, work band as set.

BODY

Set Up Row: (RS) Work 4 sts of button band as set, knit to last 4 sts increasing (+) or decreasing(-) as follows: +2 (+2, +6, -6, -6, -2) sts, work buttonhole band as set. - 184 (200, 216, 216, 232, 248) sts.

Next Row: Work 4 sts of band as set, purl to last 4 sts, work band as set.

SNOWFLAKE CHART

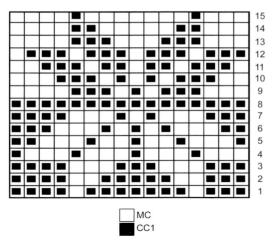

☐ MC
■ CC1

Note: Read odd numbered rows (right side rows) from right to left and read even numbered rows (wrong side rows) from left to right.

Work Chart (above) as follows:

Rows 1, 3, 5, 7: (RS) With CC1 work 4 sts of Button band as set, work Chart in knit to last 4 sts, with CC1 work buttonhole band as set.

Rows 2, 4, 6, 8: (WS) With CC1 work 4 sts of band as set, work Chart in purl to last 4 sts, with CC1 work band as set.

Rows 9, 11, 13, 15: (RS) With MC work 4 sts of button band as set, work Chart in knit to last 4 sts, with MC work buttonhole band as set.

Rows 10, 12, 14: (WS) With MC work 4 sts of band as set, work Chart in purl to last 4 sts, with MC work band as set.

Note: Chart ends with a right side row (Row 15).

Continue with Body and front bands in Main Colour:

Next Row: (WS) With MC, work 4 sts of band as set, purl to last 4 sts, work band as set.

Next Row: (RS) Work 4 sts of button band as set, knit to last 4 sts increasing evenly 0 (0, 0, 8, 8, 0) sts to last 4 sts, work button-hole band as set. - 184, (200, 216, 224, 240, 248) sts

Next Row: Work 4 sts of band as set, purl to last 4 sts, work band as set.

Work even until cardigan measures 19"/48 cm from base of neckband or 3"/7.5 cm short of desired length.

BOTTOM RIB

Row 1: (RS) Work 4 sts of button band as set, knit to last 4 sts decreasing 20 sts evenly, work buttonhole band as set. - 164 (180, 196, 204, 220, 228) sts

Row 2: Work 4 sts of band as set, purl to last 4 sts, work band as set.

Row 3: *With smaller circular needle*, work 4 sts of button band as set, work [K2, P2] rib to last 4 sts, work buttonhole band as set.

Row 4: Work 4 sts of band as set, work rib as set to last 4 sts, work band as set.

Repeat last 2 rows for 3"/7.5 cm or desired length.

Cast Off in ribbing pattern.

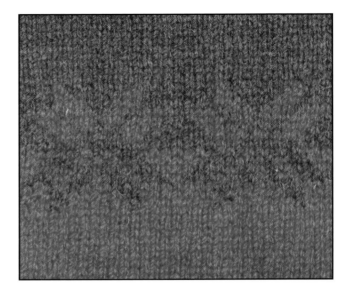

SLEEVES

Sleeve Set-Up: *With shorter circular needle*, and CC1, starting at the centre of underarm sts, attach yarn and pick up and knit 5 (6, 6, 6, 7, 7) sts from underarm cast on sts, pick up one extra st to close gap, knit around 60 (64, 68, 70, 72, 74) sleeve sts, pick up and knit one extra st to close gap, pick up and knit 4 (5, 5, 5, 6, 6) sts, join in the round and Place Marker. - 71 (77, 81, 83, 87, 89) sts

Next Round: K4 (5, 5, 5, 6, 6), K2tog, knit around sleeve sts to 5 (6, 6, 6, 7, 7) sts from end of round, SSK, knit to end of round. - 69 (75, 79, 81, 85, 87) sts

Set up Round for Chart: Knit around increasing(+) or decreasing(-) evenly as follows: -5 (+5, +1, -1, -5, -7) sts. - 64 (80, 80, 80, 80, 80) sts

Work Chart (previous page) as follows: Work the entire Chart in the round - read ALL rows of chart from RIGHT TO LEFT for every round.

Continue Sleeves in MC:

Next Round: With MC, Knit.

Decrease Round: K1, SSK, knit to last 2 sts, K2tog.

Knit 5 rounds even.

Repeat last 6 rounds until sleeve measures 14"/36 cm or 3"/7.5 cm short of desired sleeve length. Do not decrease to less than 44 (44, 44, 48, 48, 48) sts, if necessary knit even to desired sleeve length before cuff.

CUFF

Round 1: *With smaller double point needles*, knit, decreasing to 44 (44, 44, 48, 48, 48) sts if necessary.

Round 2: Work [K2, P2] to end of round.

Repeat last round for 3"/7.5 cm or desired length.

Cast Off in rib pattern.

It's All About Me!

An adaptation of the Basic Aran V-Neck by Karen Lawrence

It's all about you ... and that's as it should be.

Call it playful, exuberant, elegant or racy, this creation is just plain fun!

- *Aran (heavy worsted) weight;*

- *V-neck with collar;*

- *cropped length;*

- *bell sleeves.*

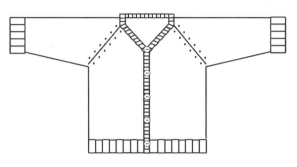

Experience Level: Intermediate

To Fit Adult Chest Size of:	35" 89 cm	38" 97 cm	40" 102 cm	43" 109 cm	46" 117 cm	49" 124 cm
FINISHED SWEATER SIZE:	39" 99 cm	42" 107 cm	45" 114 cm	47½" 121 cm	51" 130 cm	54" 137 cm

Materials: Pink Colourway: *Aran yarn - 50g ball, 98 m/108 yds*
- 4 ring markers
- 4 or 5 buttons depending on size

Pink	14	15	17	19	21	23

Needles:
5.0mm/US8 circular needles in 2 lengths (30"/80 cm long for Body and 16"/40 cm long for sleeves)

Tension:
18 sts = 4"/10 cm on 5.0mm/US8 needle in stocking stitch or needle needed to obtain this tension.

Sample knit in #8024, Extra Stampato Merino.

Designer Note: This sweater is meant to be fun and light-hearted. It is also meant to be a cropped jacket suitable for jeans or dress up. As it is so hard to pinpoint where this sweater will best sit on all body types it will be necessary to try it on while you knit it to make sure it fits you the way you would like it to.

If you need the body to be longer that's fine, please take the liberty to do so keeping in mind that your yarn requirements will change accordingly.

- Karen

ML1: MAKE LOOP: The loops form on the Right Side of the garment but are worked on the Wrong Side rows.

With wrong side of work facing: Make a loop by inserting the right-hand needle into the next stitch as if to knit, working clockwise - lay the yarn over the right-hand needle, around one finger of the left hand and return to lay over the right-hand needle again. (The yarn is wrapped around one finger and two strands of yarn are now sitting on top of the right-hand needle.) Finish knit stitch by drawing both strands on right-hand needle through the stitch originating on the left-hand needle. Replace the 2 strands back onto left-hand needle and knit together through back loop, while the loop over the left finger pulls the loop tight. Your finger should then drop the loop to the back of work (loops fall on Right Side of garment).

Note: The process of pulling the double strand through and then knitting the double strand through the back loop "locks" the stitch in place. If at times the loop may appear to "get lost", a simple tug on the loop will make it re-appear.

Note: Collar, yoke and body are worked on a circular needle, working back and forth. The sleeves are worked on a circular needle in the round.

BEGIN WITH THE COLLAR

With circular needle, **Cast On** 122 (130, 136, 138, 140, 144) sts.

Row 1: (RS) Knit.

Row 2: (WS) *K1, ML1; repeat from * to end of row.

Row 3: (RS) Knit.

Row 4: (WS) *ML1, K1; repeat from * to end of row.

Repeat last 4 rows until collar measures 3"/7.5 cm, ending with a wrong side row.

Next Row: (RS) Knit, decreasing 20 (22, 22, 22, 22, 24) sts evenly. - 102 (108, 114, 116, 118, 120) sts

The picture above shows the Wrong Side of the collar after the loops are made.

Next Row: K2tog, all the way across row. - 51 (54, 57, 58, 59, 60) sts

Next Row: Kf/b, all the way across row. - 102 (108, 114, 116, 118, 120) sts

Note: The collar of the cardigan is flipped over when worn and with the looped right side of the collar showing. The right side (RS) for the rest of the cardigan is indicated in the instructions below.

YOKE

In this sweater the Front bands for the buttons and buttonholes are cast on after the shaping for the V-Neck is completed.

The Yoke is shaped by working a pair of increases at each of 4 Markers every other row, giving the yoke it's distinctive raglan lines.

In the first row below you will place 4 raglan Markers and work the first set of increases.

Note: Each of the 4 raglan Markers is set between 2 knit sts. At each Marker, these 2 knit sts separate a pair of increases. Each Increase Row adds 8 sts to the sweater yoke.

SHORT ROW SHAPING FOR V-NECK

Short Rows are used to shape the V-neck of the cardigan. They are so named because you only work part way across the row, then turn, leaving the rest of the sts in the row unworked on the needle. The short rows chosen for this project give a smooth angle to the side of the V-neck. The short rows are worked below:

Increase SHORT Row 1: (RS) K26 (28, 30, 32, 34, 36), M1, K1, Place Marker#1, K1, M1, K8 (8, 8, 6, 4, 2), M1, K1, Place Marker#2, K1, M1, K26 (28, 30, 32, 34, 36), M1, K1, Place Marker#3, K1, M1, K8 (8, 8, 6, 4, 2), M1, K1, Place Marker#4, K1, M1, *SSK, K1, TURN.*

Wrong Side SHORT Row 2: SL1, purl to Marker#1, slip Marker, P2, *P2tog, P1, TURN.*

Increase SHORT Row 3: (RS) SL1, *knit to one stitch before Marker, M1, K1, slip Marker, K1, M1; repeat from * 3 more times, knit to one stitch before the gap, *SSK, K1, TURN.*

Wrong Side SHORT Row 4: SL1, purl around past Marker#1 to one stitch before the gap, *P2tog, P1, TURN.*

Repeat SHORT Rows 3 & 4, 10 (11, 12, 13, 14, 15) more times, until one stitch is left unworked at both ends of needle.

Last Increase SHORT Row: (RS) SL1, *knit to one stitch before Marker, M1, K1, slip Marker, K1, M1; repeat from * 3 more times, knit to one stitch before the gap, *SSK.*

Last Wrong Side SHORT Row: Purl around past Marker#1 to one stitch before the gap, *P2tog.*

Short Row shaping is complete!

All rows will now be worked across all sts on needle.

CONTINUE WITH YOKE: In the first 2 rows, Cast On stitches for Front bands.

Increase Row 1: (RS) **Cast On** 6 sts (button band), knit the 6 cast on sts, *knit to one stitch before the Marker, M1, K1, slip Marker, K1, M1; repeat from * 3 more times, knit to end of row.

Straight Row 2: **Cast On** 6 sts (band), knit the 6 cast on sts, purl to last 6 sts, K6 (band).

Increase Row 3: (RS) K6 (button band), *knit to one stitch before the Marker, M1, K1, slip Marker, K1, M1; repeat from * 3 more times, knit to last 6 sts, K6 (buttonhole band).

Straight Row 4: K6 (band), purl to last 6 sts, K6 (band).

Increase Row 5: (RS) K6 (button band), *knit to one stitch before the Marker, M1, K1, slip Marker, K1, M1; repeat from * 3 more times, knit to last 6 sts, K6 (buttonhole band).

Straight Row 6: K6 (band), purl to last 6 sts, K6 (band).

Work Buttonhole Row on next row.

Work Row 6.

> **Buttonhole Row:** (RS) K6 (button band), work in pattern as set to last 6 sts, K2, YO, K2tog, K2 (buttonhole band).

Repeat Rows 5 and 6 working a Buttonhole Row every 10th row (or 5th ridge of buttonhole band) until 288 (308, 328, 344, 360, 376) sts on needle.

Reality Check: Number of stitches between Markers: Both Fronts have 45 (48, 51, 54, 57, 60) sts, sleeves have 60 (64, 68, 70, 72, 74) sts, Back has 78 (84, 90, 96, 102, 108) sts.

Work 6 (6, 6, 4, 4, 4) rows with no further increasing, continuing to work buttonholes as set. You may lengthen yoke depth by working further rows even, if desired, continuing to make buttonholes as set. (You still have 288, 308, 328, 344, 360, 376 sts.)

Divide for Sleeves and Body: With right side facing, work 6 sts of button band as set, K39 (42, 45, 48, 51, 54) sts to first raglan Marker, remove Marker, place next 60 (64, 68, 70, 72, 74) sts of sleeve on spare yarn, remove Marker, Cast On 9 (11, 11, 11, 13, 13) sts for underarm, K78 (84, 90, 96, 102, 108) sts of Back, remove Marker, place next 60 (64, 68, 70, 72, 74) sts of sleeve on spare yarn, remove Marker, Cast On 9 (11, 11, 11, 13, 13) sts for under-

arm, K39 (42, 45, 48, 51, 54) sts to last 6 sts, work buttonhole band as set. - 186 (202, 214, 226, 242, 254) sts on circular needle for BODY.

BODY

Next Row (place new Markers): With wrong side facing, work 6 sts of band as set, purl across Front to underarm cast on sts in last row, P4 (5, 5, 5, 6, 6) to centre st, place one Marker before centre st, purl one centre st, place another Marker after centre st, purl remaining underarm sts, purl across Back to underarm sts, purl to centre st, place one Marker, purl one centre st, place Marker, purl to last 6 sts of row, work band as set.

Reality Check: There should be 4 markers in the body of the sweater, one on either side of each of the centre underarm sts.

Continue to place buttonholes as set.

Row 1: Work 6 sts of button band as set, knit to last 6 sts, work buttonhole band as set.

Row 2: Work 6 sts of band as set, purl to last 6 sts, work band as set.

Repeat last 2 rows to next buttonhole placement, work Buttonhole Row and a Row 2.

Note: The Body of the sweater should sit just below the bust. For a larger busted woman you may want to work one more buttonhole.

Buttonholes are now finished!

Repeat last 2 rows twice more.

GARTER STITCH RIDGE:

Knit 6 rows even.

NEW EDGINGS: Left Front band is in slip stitch, Right Front band has loops.

Note: SL1 with yarn in back.

Row 1: (RS) [SL1, P1] 3 times, knit to underarm marker, M1 before marker, slip

It's All About Me!

marker, K1, slip marker, M1, knit to next marker, M1 before marker, slip marker, K1, slip marker, M1, knit to last 6 sts, K6.

Row 2: [K1, ML1] 3 times, purl to last 6 sts, [SL1, P1] 3 times.

Row 3: (RS) [SL1, P1] 3 times, knit to last 6 sts, K6.

Row 4: (WS) [ML1, K1] 3 times, purl to last 6 sts, [SL1, P1] 3 times.

Repeat last 4 rows until garment sits about 1"/2.5 cm above the hip or desired length before bottom loop border (the pink version is 6"/15 cm and the green/blue version is slightly longer at 8"/20 cm), ending with a Row 4.

BOTTOM LOOP BORDER

Row 1: (RS) [SL1, P1] 3 times, knit to last 6 sts, K6.

Row 2: (WS) [K1, ML1] 3 times, work [K1, ML1] to last 6 sts, [SL1, P1] 3 times.

Row 3: [SL1, P1] 3 times, knit to last 6 sts, K6.

Row 4: (WS) [ML1, K1] 3 times, work [ML1, K1] to last 6 sts, [SL1, P1] 3 times.

Repeat last 4 rows once more.

Cast Off knitwise.

SLEEVES

Sleeve Set-Up: *With shorter circular needle,* starting at the centre of underarm cast on sts, attach yarn and pick up and knit 5 (6, 6, 6, 7, 7) sts from underarm cast on sts, pick up one extra st to close gap, knit around 60 (64, 68, 70, 72, 74) sleeves sts, pick up and knit one extra st to close gap, pick up and knit 4 (5, 5, 5, 6, 6) sts, join in the round and Place Marker. - 71 (77, 81, 83, 87, 89) sts

Sample knit in Karen's own hand-painted cotton, Windermere.

Next Round: K4 (5, 5, 5, 6, 6), K2tog, knit around sleeve sts to 5 (6, 6, 6, 7, 7) sts from end of round, SSK, knit to end of round. - 69 (75, 79, 81, 85, 87) sts

Knit 3 rounds even.

Decrease Round: K1, K2tog, knit to 2 sts before marker, SSK.

Repeat last 4 rounds until 59 (65, 69, 71, 75, 77) sts.

Knit 3 rounds even.

Increase Round: K1, M1, knit to end of round, M1.

Repeat last 4 rounds until 91 (97, 101, 103, 107, 109) sts.

Knit every round, with no further increases, until 1"/2.5 cm short of desired sleeve length.

CUFF

Decrease Round: Knit, decreasing 1 stitch in this round. - 90 (96, 100, 102, 106, 108) sts

TURN work so that PURL SIDE of sleeve is facing you and **with Wrong Side facing work ALL the following rounds:**

Round 1: Work [ML1, K1] to end of round.

Round 2: Purl.

Round 3: Work [K1, ML1] to end of round.

Round 4: Purl.

Repeat 4 rounds once more.

With wrong side facing, cast off purlwise.

FINISH

Sew in all ends, making sure to close in any gaps at underarm and at the point in the sleeve where loop pattern begins at cuff. Sew the corresponding number of buttons required onto the left hand side of the yoke opposite the buttonholes on the right hand side.

A HINT OF LACE

An adaptation of the DK Basic Crew Neck by Megan Lacey

Soft and subtle shading flows across the scalloped lace border of this delicate sweater.

- *DK weight;*
- *crew neck;*
- *hip lenght;*
- *long sleeves;*
- *buttons every 5th repeat.*

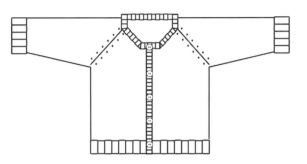

Experience Level:
Intermediate/Advanced

To Fit Adult Chest Size of:	35" 89 cm	38" 97 cm	40" 102 cm	43" 109 cm	46" 117 cm	49" 124 cm
FINISHED SWEATER SIZE:	39" 99 cm	42" 106.5 cm	44" 112 cm	47" 119.5 cm	50½" 128.5 cm	53½" 136 cm

Materials: Blue Colour Way: *DK yarn - 50g ball, 170m/184yds*
- 4 ring markers
- 8 to 9 buttons depending on the length

Colour A	5	6	6	6	7	7
Colour B	1	1	1	1	1	1
Colour C	1	1	1	1	1	1
Contrast Colour	1	1	1	1	1	1

Needles:
3.5mm/US4 circular needle (24"/60 cm long) for collar and rib bottom edge
3.5mm/US4 double pointed needles for cuffs
4.0mm/US6 circular needles in 2 lengths (30"/80 cm long for Body and 16"/40 cm long for sleeves)

Tension:
22 sts = 4"/10 cm on 4.0mm/US6 needle in stocking stitch or needle needed to obtain this tension.

Sample knit in Blue Knight, Nordic Blue, Winter Blue and Spring Green, Nature Spun.

BEGIN WITH THE NECKBAND

The first and last 4 sts of the neckband will become the Front bands for the Cardigan. The first Buttonhole is placed in the neckband.

Note: Cast on the neckband with a larger circular needle to prevent the neckband from pulling in. Work the neckband itself with a smaller circular needle. Set up the Yoke by working the last row of the neckband with the larger circular needle.

With larger circular needle and Colour A, **Cast On** 114 (118, 122, 122, 122, 122) sts.

Row 1: (RS) With smaller circular needle, work [K2, P2] to last 2 sts, K2.

Row 2: P2, work [K2, P2] to end of row.

Repeat last 2 rows for ¾"/2 cm.

Place first buttonhole in right buttonhole band in next row as follows:

Next Row (Buttonhole): (RS) Work [K2, P2] to last 6 sts, K2, YO, P2tog, K2.

Last Row: *With larger circular needle,* work in rib as set, increasing 2 sts evenly. - 116 (120, 124, 124, 124, 124) sts

YOKE

The Yoke is shaped by placing 4 Markers and working a pair of increases at each of these Markers every other row, giving the yoke it's distinctive raglan lines.

In the first row below you will place 4 raglan Markers, work the first set of increases and begin the SHORT Row shaping for the Crew Neck.

Continue to work with the larger circular needle.

Note: Each of the 4 raglan Markers is set between 2 knit sts. These 2 knit sts separate a pair of increases which are worked at each Marker. Each Increase Row adds 8 sts to the sweater yoke.

SHORT ROW SHAPING FOR CREW NECK

Short Rows are used to lower the Front of the cardigan. They are so named because you only work part way across the row, then turn, leaving the rest of the sts in the row unworked on the needle. The short rows chosen for this project give a smooth angle to the side of the crew neck. Short rows are worked below:

Increase SHORT Row 1: (RS) K28 (29, 30, 31, 32, 33), M1, K1, Place Marker#1, K1, M1, K10 (10, 10, 8, 6, 4), M1, K1, Place Marker#2, K1, M1, K32 (34, 36, 38, 40, 42), M1, K1, Place Marker#3, K1, M1, K10 (10, 10, 8, 6, 4), M1, K1, Place Marker#4, K1, M1, *SSK, K1, TURN.*

Wrong Side SHORT Row 2: SL1, purl to Marker#1, slip Marker, P2, *P2tog, P1, TURN.*

Increase SHORT Row 3: (RS) SL1, *knit to one stitch before Marker, M1, K1, slip Marker, K1, M1; repeat from * 3 more times, knit to one stitch before the gap, *SSK, K1, TURN.*

Wrong Side SHORT Row 4: SL1, purl around past Marker#1 to 1 stitch before the gap, *P2tog, P1, TURN.*

Repeat SHORT Rows 3 & 4, five more times.

Last Increase SHORT Row: (RS) SL1, *knit to one stitch before Marker, M1, K1, slip Marker, K1, M1; repeat from * 3 more times, knit to one stitch before the gap, *SSK, KNIT TO END OF ROW.*

Last Wrong Side SHORT Row: Purl around past Marker#1 to one stitch before the gap, *P2tog, PURL TO END OF ROW.*

Short Row shaping is complete! *All rows will now be worked across all sts on needle.*

CONTINUE WITH YOKE: *First and last 4 sts of each row are front band sts.*

Increase Row 1: P4 (button band), *Knit to one stitch before the Marker, M1, K1, slip Marker, K1, M1; repeat from * 3 more times, knit to last 4 sts, P4 (buttonhole band).

Straight Row 2: K4 (band), purl to last 4 sts, K4 (band).

Increase Row 3: K4 (button band), *Knit to one stitch before the Marker, M1, K1, slip Marker, K1, M1; repeat from * 3 more times, knit to last 4 sts, K4 (buttonhole band).

Straight Row 4: P4 (band), purl to last 4 sts, P4 (band).

Increase Row 5: P4 (button band), *Knit to one stitch before the Marker, M1, K1, slip Marker, K1, M1; repeat from * 3 more times, knit to last 4 sts, P4 (buttonhole band).

Straight Row 6: K4 (band), purl to last 4 sts, K4 (band).

Repeat Rows 3-6 twice more.

In next repeat of Rows 3-6 place the second buttonhole by working the Buttonhole Row instead of Row 3, as follows:

Buttonhole Row: (substitute for Row 3): K4 (button band), *Knit to one stitch before the Marker, M1, K1, slip Marker, K1, M1; repeat from * 3 more times, knit to last 4 sts, K1, YO, K2tog, K1 (buttonhole band).

Note: Buttonhole placement is different than in the neckband.

Work Rows 4, 5, & 6 above.

Repeat Rows 3-6 above, until 356 (376, 396, 420, 444, 468) sts on needle, *working a Buttonhole Row instead of Row 3 in every following 5th repeat* of Rows 3-6.

Reality Check: Number of stitches between Markers: Both Fronts have 53 (56, 59, 63, 67, 71) sts, sleeves have 76 (80, 84, 88, 92, 96) sts, Back has 98 (104, 110, 118, 126, 134) sts.

Work 6 (6, 6, 4, 4, 4) rows even with no further increasing, continuing the front bands as established. You may lengthen Yoke depth by working extra rows even, if desired. (You still have 356, 376, 396, 420, 444, 468 sts.)

Divide for Sleeves and Body: With right side facing, work 4 sts of button band as set, K49 (52, 55, 59, 63, 67) sts to first raglan Marker, remove Marker, place next 76 (80, 84, 88, 92, 96) sts of sleeve on spare yarn, remove Marker, Cast On 9 (11, 11, 11, 13, 13) sts for underarm, K98 (104, 110, 118, 126, 134) sts of Back, place next 76 (80, 84, 88, 92, 96) sts of sleeve on spare yarn, remove Marker, Cast On 9 (11, 11, 11, 13, 13) sts for underarm, K49 (52, 55, 59, 63, 67) sts to last 4 sts, work buttonhole band as set. - 222 (238, 250, 266, 286, 302) sts on circular needle for BODY.

Next Row: (WS) Work 4 sts of band as set, purl to last 4 sts, work band as set.

BODY

Row 1: (RS) Work 4 sts of button band as set, knit to last 4 sts, work buttonhole band as set.

Row 2: (WS) Work 4 sts of band as set, purl to last 4 sts, work band as set.

Repeat last 2 rows until cardigan measures 16 (16, 17, 17, 18, 18)"/41 (41, 43, 43, 46, 46) cm from bottom of neckband or 6"/15 cm short of desired length, ending after a Row 2.

Continue to work buttonholes as established!

FAIRISLE PATTERN:

Set-Up Row: (RS) Work 4 sts of button band as set, knit to last 4 sts increasing(+) and decreasing(-) as follows: +2 (-2, -2, -6, -2, -6) sts, work 4 sts of buttonhole band as set. - 224 (236, 248, 260, 284, 296) sts

Next Row: Work 4 sts of band as set, purl to last 4 sts, work band as set.

Work 11 rows of FAIRISLE CHART, maintaining front bands in Colour A as established, ending with right side row.

FAIRISLE CHART

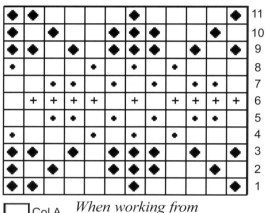

When working from FAIRISLE CHART, read odd numbered rows (Right side rows) from right to left and even numbered rows (Wrong side rows) from left to right.

Note: *Chart ends with a Right Side Row.*

Next Row: (WS) With Colour A, work 4 sts of band as set, purl to last 4 sts, work band as set.

LACE BORDER

Note: The Front bands are maintained in Colour A. You will have to wind a small ball of Colour A yarn for knitting the second Front band for the duration of the Lace Panel.
Set-Up Row: (RS) Work 4 sts of button band as set, knit to last 4 sts, increasing(+) and decreasing(-) as follows: +4 (+3, +2, +1, -1, -2) sts, work buttonhole band as set. - 228 (239, 250, 261, 283, 294) sts.

WORK LACE PATTERN below *changing colours* according to the COLOUR SEQUENCE in box, maintaining the Front bands in Colour A, and continuing to work buttonholes as established.

LACE PATTERN:

Note: All colour changes begin on Wrong Side Row.

Row 1: (WS) Work 4 sts of band as set, purl to last 4 sts, work band as set.

Row 2: (RS) Work 4 sts of button band as set, *K2tog, K3, YO, K1, YO, K3, K2tog; repeat from * to last 4 sts, work buttonhole band as set.

Row 3: (WS) Work 4 sts of band as set, Knit to last 4 sts, work band as set.

Row 4: (RS) Work 4 sts of button band as set, Purl to last 4 sts, work buttonhole band as set.

Sample knit in Walnut, Soft Pink and Birch, Cotton Tweed DK.

SLEEVES

The sleeves are meant to be a little longer than normal so that the sleeve sits about 1½"/4 cm past the wrist. But the finished sleeve length is of course totally up to you.

Sleeve Set-Up: Starting at the centre of underarm cast on sts, attach Colour A and pick up and knit 5 (6, 6, 6, 7, 7) sts from underarm cast on sts, pick up one extra st to close gap, knit around 76 (80, 84, 88, 92, 96) sleeve sts, pick up and knit one extra st to close gap, pick up and knit 4 (5, 5, 5, 6, 6) sts, join in the round and Place Marker. - 87 (93, 97, 101, 107, 111) sts

Next Round: K4 (5, 5, 5, 6, 6), K2tog, knit around to 5 (6, 6, 6, 7, 7) sts from end of round, SSK, knit to end of round. - 85 (91, 95, 99, 105, 109) sts

Knit 4 (4, 4, 8, 12) rounds even.

Decrease Round: K1, SSK, knit to last 2 sts, K2tog.

Knit 5 (4, 4, 3, 3, 3) rounds even.

Repeat last 6 (5, 5, 4, 4, 4) rounds until sleeve is 12"/30 cm long or 6"/15 cm short of desired sleeve length (6"/15 cm cuff is worked next). Do Not decrease to less than 61 sts, if necessary work straight to desired length before cuff.

Change to double pointed needles when necessary.

FAIRISLE PATTERN:

Set-Up Round: Knit around, decreasing 1 st on next round. - 60 sts.

Work 11 rounds of FAIRISLE CHART.

Note: When working chart in the round always read All Rows from right to left.

Next Round: With Colour A, knit.

LACE BORDER

Set-Up Round: Knit around, decreasing 5 sts evenly. - 55 sts.

WORK LACE PATTERN below *changing colours* according to the COLOUR SEQUENCE in box.

LACE PATTERN (Worked in the round)

Round 1: Knit.

Round 2: *K2tog, K3, YO, K1, YO, K3, K2tog; repeat from * to end of round.

Round 3: Purl.

Round 4: Purl.

Work 4 Rounds of Lace Pattern in colour sequence below:

COLOUR SEQUENCE
With Colour A, work Rounds 1 and 2 of LACE PATTERN, 3 times.
With Colour A, work Rounds 3 and 4 of LACE PATTERN, once.
With Colour B, work Rounds 1 and 2 of LACE PATTERN, 3 times.
With Colour B, work Rounds 3 and 4 of LACE PATTERN, once.
With Colour C, work Rounds 1 and 2 of LACE PATTERN, 4 times.
With Contrast Colour, work Rounds 1 and 2 of LACE PATTERN, once.
With Colour C, work Rounds 1 and 2 of LACE PATTERN, once.
With Colour C, work Rounds 3 and 4 of LACE PATTERN, 3 times.
With Colour C, Cast Off all sts.

FINISHING

Sew in all ends. Sew buttons in place. Wear and enjoy.

THE SARAH

An adaptation of the Basic DK V-Neck by Bernice Vollick

A contemporary look with up-to-the minute fashion touches. The generous collar flatters the face and invites jewellery, while the eye-catching cable medallion at the back nips in the waist.

- DK weight;
- V-neck;
- long sleeve;
- zipper closure.

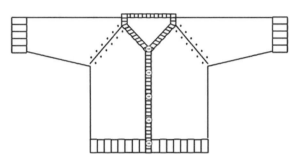

Experience Level:
Intermediate/Advanced

To Fit Adult Chest Size of:	35" 89 cm	38" 97 cm	40" 102 cm	43" 109 cm	46" 117 cm	49" 124 cm
FINISHED SWEATER SIZE:	39" 99 cm	42" 107 cm	45" 114 cm	48" 122 cm	50½" 128 cm	53½" 134 cm

Materials DK yarn - 50g ball, 105 m/115 yds
- 4 ring markers
- zipper (16"/40 cm or 18"/46 cm or length needed to reach from the bottom of the ribbing to the neck band.)

Periwinkle	12	13	13	14	14	15

Materials: : DK yarn - 100g ball, 230m/250yds

Red	6	6	7	7	7	7

Needles:
4.5mm/US7 circular needle (24"/60 cm long) for the Collar ONLY
3.25mm/US3 circular needle (24"/60 cm long) for the Collar shaping ONLY
3.75mm/US5 circular needles in 2 lengths (16"/40 cm and 24"/60 cm long)
Set of 3.75mm/US5 double pointed needles for sleeve.

Tension:
22 sts = 4"/10 cm on 3.75mm/US5 needle in stocking stitch or needle needed to obtain this tension.

Sample knit in #142 Ruma 3 tr. Strikke-garn.

The Sarah

Note: Collar, Yoke and Body are worked on circular needle, working back and forth. The sleeves are worked on a circular needle in the round.

BEGIN WITH THE COLLAR

The first and last 4 sts of each row form a seed stitch band which become the Front band sts for the zipper of the sweater.

With larger circular needle Cast On 166 (166, 166, 176, 176, 176) sts.

Work back and forth on circular needle:

Row 1: (RS) K2, P1, K1 (band), work [K3, P2] to last 7 sts, K3, (band) K1, P1, K1, wyif SL1(p).

Row 2: (WS) K2, P1, K1 (band), work [P3, K2] to last 7 sts, P3, (band) K1, P1, K1, wyif SL1(p).

Repeat Rows 1 & 2 until work from cast on edge measures 5"/13 cm, ending after a WS row.

COLLAR SHAPING

Change to smallest circular needle (24"/60 cm long).

Row 3: (RS) K2, P1, K1 (band), work [K3, P2tog] to last 7 sts, K3, (band) K1, P1, K1, wyif SL1(p). - 135 (135, 135, 143, 143, 143) sts.

Row 4: K2, P1, K1 (band), work [P3, K1] to last 7 sts, P3, (band) K1, P1, K1, wyif SL1(p).

Row 5: (RS) K2, P1, K1 (band), work [K3, P1] to last 7 sts, K3, (band) K1, P1, K1, wyif SL1(p) (band).

Row 6: K2, P1, K1 (band), work [P3, K1] to last 7 sts, P3, (band) K1, P1, K1, wyif SL1(p).

Rows 7 - 10: Repeat Rows 5 and 6, twice more.

Change to 3.75mm/US5 circular needle (24"/60 cm long).

Last (Marker) Row: (RS) K2, P1, K1 (band), K33 (33, 33, 37, 37, 37), Place Marker, K13 (13, 13, 9, 9, 9), Place Marker, K35 (35, 35, 43, 43, 43), Place Marker, K13 (13, 13, 9, 9, 9), Place Marker, K33 (33, 33, 37, 37, 37), K1, P1, K1, wyif SL1(p) (band).

Collar is flipped over when worn so that the right side rows are seen. The right side (RS) for the sweater is indicated in the instructions below.

YOKE

The Yoke is shaped by working a pair of increases at each of the 4 markers every other row, giving the yoke it's distinctive raglan lines. Each of the 4 raglan Markers is set between 2 knit sts which separate the pair of increases. In the first row below you will work the first set of increases.

Please Note: Each Increase Row adds 8 sts to the sweater yoke.

This sweater has a centre 25 stitch ribbed panel which runs down the centre Back and down both sleeves. The Front of the sweater is plain and worked in stockinette stitch. As you work the V-neck shaping below you will also be establishing these centre rib panels in the Back and on both sleeves.

Instructions are given for Sizes 39 (42, 45)"/99 (107, 114) cm below and Sizes 48 (50½, 53½)"/122 (128.5, 136) cm separately on page 92.

SIZES 39 (42, 44)"/99 (107, 112) cm ONLY:

SHORT ROW SHAPING FOR V-NECK

Short Rows are used to shape the V-neck of the cardigan. They are so named because you only work part way across the row, then turn, leaving the rest of the sts in the row unworked on the needle. The short rows chosen for this project give a smooth angle to the side of the V-neck. The short rows are worked below:

Increase SHORT Row 1: (RS of Body of cardigan) K2, P1, K1, knit to one stitch before the Marker, M1, K1, slip Marker, K1, M1, K1, work [P1, K3] twice, P1, K1, M1, K1, slip Marker, K1, M1, K4, work [P1, K3] 6 times, P1, K4, M1, K1, slip Marker, K1, M1, K1, work [P1, K3] twice, P1, K1, M1, K1, slip Marker, K1, M1, *SSK, K1, Turn.*

Wrong Side SHORT Row 2: SL1, purl to first Marker, slip Marker, P3, work [K1, P3] 3 times, slip Marker, P6, work [K1, P3] 6 times, K1, purl to next Marker, slip Marker, P3, [K1, P3] 3 times, slip Marker, P2, *P2tog, P1, Turn.*

Increase SHORT Row 3: SL1, knit to one stitch before the Marker, M1, K1, slip Marker, K1, M1, K2, work [P1, K3] twice, P1, K2, M1, K1, slip Marker, K1, M1, K5, work [P1, K3] 6 times, P1, K5, M1, K1, slip Marker, K1, M1, K2, work [P1, K3] twice, P1, K2, M1, K1, slip Marker, K1, M1, knit to one stitch before the gap, *SSK, K1, Turn.*

Wrong side SHORT Row 4: SL1, purl to first Marker, slip Marker, P4, work [K1, P3] twice, K1, P4, slip Marker, P7, work [K1, P3] 6 times, K1, purl to next Marker, slip Marker, P4, work [K1, P3] twice, K1, P4, slip Marker, purl to one st before the gap, *P2tog, P1, Turn.*

Increase SHORT Row 5: SL1, knit to one stitch before the Marker, M1, K1, slip Marker, K1, M1, K3, work [P1, K3] 3 times, M1, K1, slip Marker, K1, M1, K6, work [P1, K3] 6 times, P1, K6, M1, K1, slip Marker, K1, M1, K3, work [P1, K3] 3 times, M1, K1, slip Marker, K1, M1, knit to one stitch before the gap, *SSK, K1, Turn.*

Wrong side SHORT Row 6: SL1, purl to first Marker, slip Marker, P5, work [K1, P3] twice, K1, P5, slip Marker, P8, work [K1, P3] 6 times, K1, purl to next Marker, slip Marker, P5, work [K1, P3] twice, K1, P5, slip Marker, purl to one st before the gap, *P2tog, P1, Turn.*

The 25 stitch centre ribbed panel is now well established on the Back.

Increase SHORT Row 7: SL1, knit t to one stitch before the Marker, M1, K1, slip Marker, K1, M1, work [P1, K3] 4 times, P1, M1, K1, slip Marker, K1, M1, K7, work rib panel, knit to one stitch before the Marker, M1, K1, slip Marker, K1, M1, work [P1, K3] 4 times, P1, M1, K1, slip Marker, K1, M1, knit to one stitch before the gap, *SSK, K1, Turn.*

Wrong side SHORT Row 8: SL1, purl to first Marker, slip Marker, P2, work [K1, P3] 4 times, K1, P2, slip Marker, purl to centre panel, work rib panel, purl to next Marker, slip Marker, P2, work [K1, P3] 4 times, K1, P2, slip Marker, purl to one stitch before the gap, *P2tog, P1, Turn.*

Increase SHORT Row 9: SL1, knit to one stitch before the Marker, M1, K1, slip Marker, K1, M1, K1, work [P1, K3] 4 times, P1, K1, M1, K1, slip Marker, K1, M1, knit to centre panel, work rib panel, knit to one stitch before the Marker, M1, K1, slip Marker, K1, M1, K1, work [P1, K3] 4 times, P1, K1, M1, K1, slip Marker, K1, M1, knit to one stitch before the gap, *SSK, K1, Turn.*

Wrong side SHORT Row 10: SL1, purl to first Marker, slip Marker, P3, work [K1, P3] 5 times, slip Marker, purl to centre panel, work rib panel, purl to next Marker, slip Marker, P3, work [K1, P3] 5 times, slip Marker, purl to one stitch before the gap, *P2tog, P1, Turn.*

Increase SHORT Row 11: SL1, knit to one stitch before the Marker, M1, K1, slip Marker, K1, M1, K2, work [P1, K3] 4 times, P1, K2, M1, K1, slip Marker, K1, M1, knit to centre panel, work rib panel, knit to one stitch before the Marker, M1, K1, slip

Marker, K1, M1, K2, work [P1, K3] 4 times, P1, K2, M1, K1, slip Marker, K1, M1, knit to one stitch before the gap, *SSK, K1, Turn.*

Wrong side SHORT Row 12: SL1, purl to first Marker, slip Marker, P4, work [K1, P3] 4 times, K1, P4, slip Marker, purl to centre panel, work rib panel, purl to next Marker, slip Marker, P4, work [K1, P3] 4 times, K1, P4, slip Marker, purl to one stitch before the gap, *P2tog, P1, Turn.*

Increase SHORT Row 13: SL1, knit to one stitch before the Marker, M1, K1, slip Marker, K1, M1, K3, work [P1, K3] 5 times, M1, K1, slip Marker, K1, M1, knit to centre panel, work rib panel, knit to one stitch before the Marker, M1, K1, slip Marker, K1, M1, K3, work [P1, K3] 5 times, M1, K1, slip Marker, K1, M1, knit to one stitch before the gap, *SSK, K1, Turn.*

Wrong side SHORT Row 14: SL1, purl to first Marker, slip Marker, P5, work [K1, P3] 4 times, K1, P5, slip Marker, purl to centre panel, work rib panel, purl to next Marker, slip Marker, P5, work [K1, P3] 4 times, K1, P5, slip Marker, purl to one stitch before the gap, *P2tog, P1, Turn.*

Increase SHORT Row 15: SL1, knit to one stitch before the Marker, M1, K1, slip Marker, K1, M1, work [P1, K3] 6 times, P1, M1, K1, slip Marker, K1, M1, knit to centre panel, work rib panel, knit to one stitch before the Marker, M1, K1, slip Marker, K1, M1, work [P1, K3] 6 times, P1, M1, K1, slip Marker, K1, M1, knit to one stitch before the gap, *SSK, K1, Turn.*

Wrong side SHORT Row 16: SL1, purl to first Marker, slip Marker, P2, work [K1, P3] 6 times, K1, P2, slip Marker, purl to centre panel, work rib panel, purl to next Marker, slip Marker, P2, work [K1, P3] 6 times, K1, P2, slip Marker, purl to one stitch before the gap, *P2tog, P1, Turn.*

The 25 stitch ribbed panel is now established on both sleeves.

Increase SHORT Row 17: SL1, knit to one stitch before the Marker, M1, K1, slip Marker, K1, M1, K1, work rib panel, K1, M1, K1, slip Marker, K1, M1, knit to centre panel, work rib panel, knit to one stitch before the Marker, M1, K1, slip Marker, K1, M1, K1, work rib panel, K1, M1, K1, slip Marker, K1, M1, knit to one stitch before the gap, *SSK, K1, Turn.*

Wrong side SHORT Row 18: SL1, purl to first Marker, slip Marker, P3, work rib panel, P3, slip Marker, purl to centre panel, work rib panel, purl to next Marker, slip Marker, P3, work rib panel, P3, slip Marker, purl to one stitch before the gap, *P2tog, P1, Turn.*

You have now established the 25 stitch ribbed panel at the centre of each sleeve and the centre Back of the cardigan.

Continue with the ALL SIZES instructions for the remaining SHORT rows on page 92.

Sample knit in Cherry Cotton Tweed DK.

The Sarah is continued on page 92.

The Sarah

CHECKMATE STRIPES

An adaptation of the Basic Aran Square Neck by Megan Lacey

Make your striping sophisticated and subtle, bold and brave or simply "play as you go". Here's your chance to have fun with colour!

- *Aran (heavy worsted) weight;*
- *square neck & long sleeves;*
- *hip length;*
- *zipper closure.*

Experience Level: With Gusto!
(Enthusiastic Beginner)

To Fit Adult Chest Size of:	35" 89 cm	38" 97 cm	40" 102 cm	43" 109 cm	46" 117 cm	49" 124 cm
FINISHED SWEATER SIZE:	39" 99 cm	42" 107 cm	44" 114 cm	47½" 121 cm	51" 130 cm	54" 137 cm

Materials: Two-Colourway: Aran yarn - 100g ball, 173m/190yds
- *4 ring markers*
- *zipper*

Main Colour (Dark)	3	3	4	4	5	5
Contrast Colour (Light)	3	3	4	4	5	5

Materials: Multi-Colourway: Aran yarn - 50g ball, 106m/116yds

Main Colour (Black)	2	2	2	2	2	2
Contrast Colour (White)	1	1	1	1	1	1
Colours 1 through 11 (11 balls, see overleaf for list of colours)	1 ea	1 ea	1 ea	1 ea	1 ea	1 ea

Needles:
4.5mm/US7 circular needle (24"/60 cm long) for collar, bottom edge and front zipper bands
4.5mm/US7 double pointed needles for cuffs
5.0mm/US8 circular needles in 2 lengths (30"/80 cm long for Body and 16"/40 cm long for sleeves)

Tension:
18 sts = 4"/10 cm on 5.0mm/US8 needle in stocking stitch or needle needed to obtain this tension.

The yarn used in the sample opposite is Medieval Red and Spice, Lamb's Pride.
Multi-colourway on following page in Manos Cotton Stria (colour chart on following page).

CheckMate Stripes

TWO COLOUR STRIPE SEQUENCE	
Main Colour: Red, Contrast Colour: Spice	
Stripe 1: 2 rows	Main Colour - Red
Stripe 2: 4 rows	Contrast Colour - Spice
Stripe 3: 2 rows	Main Colour - Red
Stripe 4: 1 row	Contrast Colour - Spice
Stripe 5: 3 rows	Main Colour - Red
Stripe 6: 1 row.	Contrast Colour - Spice (repeat)

BEGIN WITH GARTER STITCH NECKBAND.

Note: Cast on the neckband with a larger circular needle to prevent the neckband from pulling in. Work the band itself with a smaller circular needle.

With larger circular needle and Main Color, **Cast On** 76 (80, 84, 84, 84, 84) sts.

Work back and forth on circular needle:

Row 1: (RS) *With smaller circular needle,* Knit.

Repeat last row for 1"/2.5 cm, ending with Wrong Side row.

YOKE

The Yoke is shaped by placing 4 Markers and working a pair of increases at each of these markers every other row, giving the yoke it's distinctive raglan lines. Each of the 4 raglan Markers is set between 2 knit sts which separate the pair of increases.

In the first row below you will place 4 raglan Markers and work the first set of increases.

Note: Increase used was the Open M1, page 102.

BEGIN TO WORK IN STRIPES (SEE CHARTS ABOVE):

*Note: For Multi-Colour version, repeat Stripes 1 to 6, **at the same time** continuously working through Colours 1 to 11.*

Increase Row 1: (RS) *With larger circular needle,* K13 (14, 15, 16, 17, 18), M1, K1,

MULTI-COLOUR SEQUENCE	
Main Colour: Black, Contrast Colour White	
Stripe 1: 2 rows	Colour 1- Aqua
Stripe 2: 4 rows	Colour 2 - Tangerine
Stripe 3: 2 rows	Colour 3 - Pistachio
Stripe 4: 1 row	Colour 4 - Bubblegum
Stripe 5: 3 rows	Colour 5 - Lilac
Stripe 6: 1 row	Colour 6 - Violet
Stripe 1: 2 rows	Colour 7 - Navy
Stripe 2: 4 rows	Colour 8 - Olive
Stripe 3: 2 rows	Colour 9 - Spice
Stripe 4: 1 row	Colour 10 - Sky
Stripe 5: 3 rows	Color 11 - Red
Stripe 6: 1 row.	Begin Colour Sequence again with Colour 1 ...
You have more colours than stripes. ***This is intentional !*** *When the number of stripes does not divide evenly into the number of colours, a different colour sequence for each new set of stripes is created.*	

Place Marker, K1, M1, K8 (8, 8, 6, 4, 2), M1, K1, Place Marker, K1, M1, K26 (28, 30, 32, 34, 36), M1, K1, Place Marker, K1, M1, K8 (8, 8, 6, 4, 2), M1, K1, Place Marker, K1, M1, K13 (14, 15, 16, 17, 18). - 84 (88, 92, 92, 92, 92) sts on needle.

Note: Each Increase Row adds 8 sts to the sweater yoke.

Straight Row 2: Purl.

Increase Row 3: *Knit to one stitch before the Marker, M1, K1, slip Marker, K1, M1; repeat from * 3 more times, knit to end of row.

Straight Row 4: Purl.

Repeat Rows 3 & 4 until 276 (296, 316, 332, 348, 364) sts on needle.

Reality Check: *Number of stitches between Markers: Both Fronts have 39 (42, 45, 48, 51, 54) sts, sleeves have 60 (64, 68, 70, 72, 74) sts, Back has 78 (84, 90, 96, 102, 108) sts.*

Work 6 (6, 6, 4, 4, 4) rows even in Stripe Sequence, with no further increasing. You may lengthen Yoke depth by working extra rows even, if desired. You still have 276 (296, 316, 332, 348, 364) sts.

DIVIDE FOR SLEEVES AND BODY:

With right side facing, K39 (42, 45, 48, 51, 54) sts to first raglan Marker, remove Marker, place next 60 (64, 68, 70, 72, 74) sts of sleeve on spare yarn, remove Marker, Cast On 9 (11, 11, 11, 13, 13) sts for under-arm, K78 (84, 90, 96, 102, 108) sts of Back, place next 60 (64, 68, 70, 72, 74) sts of sleeve on spare yarn, remove Marker, Cast On 9 (11, 11, 11, 13, 13) sts for underarm, K39 (42, 45, 48, 51, 54) sts. - 174 (190, 202, 214, 230, 242) sts on circular needle for BODY.

Next Row: Purl.

BODY

Continue to work Stripe Pattern as set.

Row 1: Knit.

Row 2: Purl.

Repeat last 2 rows until cardigan measures 20 (20, 20, 21, 21, 21)"/51 (51, 51, 53, 53, 53) cm from bottom of neckband or 2½"/6 cm short of desired length, ending after a Row 2.

BOTTOM CHECKERBOARD PATTERN

Row 1: (RS) *With smaller circular needle and Main Color,* knit, decreasing 10 sts evenly across row. - 164 (180, 192, 204, 220, 232) sts

Knit 3 rows.

Starting with right side facing, work 8 rows of CHECKERBOARD CHART.

Note: *If you find that when knitting with 2 colours your work tightens up you could use the larger needle to work the 2 colour checkerboard chart and then return to the smaller needle for the rest of the border.*

CHECKERBOARD CHART

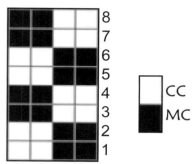

Read odd numbered rows from right to left (Right Side rows) and read even rows from left to right (Wrong Side rows).

When Chart is completed break CC1 yarn.

Next Row: (RS) With Main Color, Knit.

Knit 3 rows.

Cast Off all sts.

SLEEVES

Sleeve Set-Up: *With shorter circular needle,* work in established stripe pattern to match the body, starting at the centre of underarm cast on sts, attach yarn and pick up and knit 5 (6, 6, 6, 7, 7) sts from underarm cast on sts, pick up one extra st to close gap, knit around 60 (64, 68, 70, 72, 74) sleeves sts, pick up and knit one extra st to close gap, pick up and knit 4 (5, 5, 5, 6, 6) sts, join in the round and Place Marker. - 71 (77, 81, 83, 87, 89) sts

Next Round: K4 (5, 5, 5, 6, 6), K2tog, knit around sleeve sts to 5 (6, 6, 6, 7, 7) sts from end of round, SSK, knit to end of round. - 69 (75, 79, 81, 85, 87) sts

Knit 8 (8, 8, 6, 6, 6) rounds even.

Decrease Round: K1, SSK, knit to last 2 sts, K2tog.

Knit 5 rounds even.

Repeat last 6 rounds until sleeve is 14½"/37 cm long from underarm or 2½"/6.5 cm short of desired sleeve length. Do not decrease to less than 45 (45, 45, 49, 49, 49) sts.

CHECKERBOARD CUFF

Round 1: *With double pointed needles* and Main Color, knit around, decreasing evenly to 44 (44, 44, 48, 48, 48) sts.

Round 2: Purl.

Round 3: Knit.

Round 4: Purl.

Work 8 rounds of CHECKERBOARD pattern, reading ALL rounds from right to left.

Break CC1 yarn.

Next Round: With Main Color, Knit.

Round 2: Purl.

Repeat last 2 rounds once more.

Cast Off all sts.

FRONT ZIPPER BANDS

Right Front Band: With Main Colour, smaller circular needle and with right side facing, starting at hem, pick up and knit one stitch for each ridge of garter stitch border and 2 sts for every 3 rows up Front of cardigan to top, pick up and knit one st for each ridge of neckband.

Knit 3 rows. **Cast Off.**

Left Front Band: Starting at top of neckband work as for Right Band.

TO FINISH

Baste zipper into place and hand stitch securely. Sew in all loose ends.

Sample knit in Manos Cotton Stria

FALLING LEAVES

FALLING LEAVES

An adaptation of the Basic DK Square Neck by Dana Gibbons

This elegant garment, with its easy lace pattern can be made as long as you wish or shorter for a cropped look. Either way, it will add a dress up factor to your wardrobe.

There is very little shaping to manage with this sweater. The lace is an easy alternating mini leaf pattern.

- *DK weight;*

- *square neck & long sleeves;*

- *two lengths.*

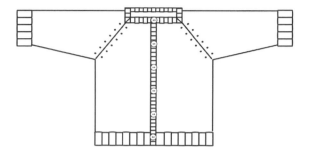

Experience Level:
Intermediate/Advanced

To Fit Adult Chest Size of:	35" 89 cm	38" 97 cm	40" 102 cm	43" 109 cm	46" 117 cm	49" 124 cm
FINISHED SWEATER SIZE:	39" 99 cm	42" 107 cm	44" 112 cm	47" 120 cm	50½" 129 cm	53½" 136 cm
Long Length:	24" 61 cm	24½" 62 cm	25" 64 cm	25" 64 cm	26½" 68 cm	27" 69 cm
Short Length:	19" 49 cm	20" 51 cm	21" 54 cm	21" 54 cm	22" 56 cm	23" 59 cm

Materials: **All colours:** *DK yarn - 100g ball, 230m/250yds*
6 Ring Markers for yoke of jacket, 10-12 Ring Markers for Corona Border Pattern
- 4 to 5 15mm buttons

Brown (Short version)	5	5	6	6	7	7
Green (Long version)	6	6	7	7	8	8

Needles:
4.0mm/US6 circular needles in 2 lengths (16"/40 cm and 30"/80 cm long)
3.25mm/US3 circular needles in 2 lengths (16"/40 cm and 30"/80 cm long)
Set of 3.25mm/US3 double pointed needles for sleeve.

Tension:
22 sts = 4"/10 cm on 4.0mm/US6 needle in stocking stitch or needle needed to obtain this tension.

Sample on previous page knit in Walnut, Tatamy Tweed.

BEGIN WITH THE SEED STITCH COLLAR

With smaller circular needle (30" long/80 cm), **Cast On** 91 (95, 99, 99, 99, 99) sts.

Next Row: Work [K1, P1] to last st, K1.

Repeat last row for 2.5"/6 cm, ending after Right Side row.

Back of Neck Ribbing:

Row 1: (WS) K1, P1, K1, P2, work [K1, P1] to last 6 sts, K1, P2, K1, P1, K1.

Row 2: Work [K1, P1] to last st, K1.

Row 3: As Row 1.

Row 4: As Row 2.

Row 5: As Row 1.

Change to larger circular needle (30"/80 cm).

Row 6: Work Row 2, increasing one stitch in the middle of the row. - 92 (96, 100, 100, 100, 100) sts.

Note: The collar of the cardigan is flipped over when worn and then the right side of the collar will be the side showing. The right side (RS) for the rest of the cardigan is indicated in the following instructions.

YOKE

In the next 2 rows, we will cast on additional sts and make 8 stitch Front bands and place 4 Markers for the raglan increases.

Note: The first 8 sts and the last 8 sts of every row are the Front bands. The first two sts and the last two sts of each Front band are the attached I-cord edging and the remaining 6 sts of each Front band are worked in seed stitch.

Tip: We recommend that you use 2 additional markers (of a different colour than the increase markers) to delineate the Front bands. The placement is indicated in Row 1 and will not be referred to in the rest of the pattern.

Increase Row 1: (RS) **Cast On** 5 sts, work K2, P1, [K1, P1] twice, K1 across 5 cast on sts and next 3 sts (for Front band), place band marker if desired, K13 (14, 15, 16, 17, 18) for Front, YO, K1, place Marker, K1, YO, K10 (10, 10, 8, 6, 4) for sleeve, YO, K1, place Marker, K1, YO, K32 (34, 36, 38, 40, 42) for Back, YO, K1, place Marker, K1, YO, K10 (10, 10, 8, 6, 4) for second sleeve, YO, K1, place Marker, K1, YO, K13 (14, 15, 16, 17, 18), place Front band marker if desired, K1, P1, K1.

> **wyif SL2(p)** - with yarn in front, slip 2 sts purlwise.

Straight Row 2: **Cast On** 5 sts, work K2, P1, [K1, P1] twice, K1 across 5 cast on sts and next 3 sts (for Front band), purl to last 8 sts slipping markers as you go, [K1, P1] 3 times, wyif SL2(p) (Front band).

Increase Row 3: (RS) Bring yarn across back of work and K2 (I-Cord edge), P1, [K1, P1] twice, K1 (band), *knit to one stitch before first marker, YO, K1, slip Marker, K1, YO; repeat from * 3 times, knit to last 8 sts, [K1, P1] 3 times, wyif SL2(p) (band).

Straight Row 4: Bring yarn across back of work and K2, P1, [K1, P1] twice, K1 (band), purl to last 8 sts, [K1, P1] 3 times, wyif SL2(p) (band).

Rows 5 - 8: Repeat Rows 3 and 4, twice more.

Increase Row 9 (Buttonhole Row): (RS) K2, P1, K1, YO, K2tog, P1, K1 (band), working increases as set, Knit to last 8 sts, K1, P1, K2tog, YO, K1, P1, wyif SL2(p) (band). *(Yes, there are buttonholes on both sides. I always do this as it makes it easier to place buttons. Simply sew the button over the holes of the Left Front band. Your buttons and buttonholes will match perfectly.)*

Straight Row 10: As Row 4.

Repeat Rows 3 & 4 until 358 (378, 398, 422, 446, 470) sts on needle, AT THE

Sample knit in Oatmeal Cotton Tweed DK.

SAME TIME, placing buttonholes every 18 (20, 20, 20, 18, 20) rows.

Reality Check: You should have 54 (57, 60, 64, 68, 72) sts for both Fronts, both sleeves should have 76 (80, 84, 88, 92, 96) sts, and 98 (104, 110, 118, 126, 134) sts across the Back.

Work 6 (6, 6, 4, 4, 4) rows even with no further increases, adding buttonholes if necessary. If deeper yoke is desired work more rows even until desired length.

Buttonholes are completed.

Dividing for sleeves and Body: (RS) Remove All Markers as you work across row, work 8 sts of band as set, K46 (49, 52, 56, 60, 64) sts to first marker (Front), put next 76 (80, 84, 88, 92, 96) sts of sleeve on spare circular needle or yarn, Cast On 7 (11, 11, 11, 13, 13) sts for underarm,

K98 (104, 110, 118, 126, 134) sts across Back, put next 76 (80, 84, 88, 92, 96) sts of sleeve on a spare needle or yarn, Cast On 7 (11, 11, 11, 13, 13) sts for underarm, K46 (49, 52, 56, 60, 64) sts, work 8 sts of band as set. - 220 (240, 252, 268, 288, 304) sts on needle for BODY.

Ridge:

Note: To accomodate the Falling Leaves pattern adjust by increasing or decreasing in the next row:

Row 1: (WS) Knit to last 2 sts, wyif SL2(p), AT THE SAME TIME increasing(+) or decreasing(-) according to size +1 (-1, -1, +1, -1, +1) stitch in the middle of the Back. - 221 (239, 251, 269, 287, 305) sts

Row 2: (RS) K2 (I-cord), purl to last 2 sts, wyif SL2(p).

Row 3: (WS) K2, purl to last 2 sts, wyif SL2(p).

Sample knit in Pale Slate Super10 Cotton.

Falling Leaves

FALLING LEAVES PATTERN:

We are going to discontinue the seed stitch part of the button bands, but maintain the I-Cord edging as follows:

Rows 1, 3, 5: K3, *YO, SSK, K1, K2tog, YO, K1; repeat from * to last 2 sts, wyif SL2(p).

Row 2 and all Wrong Side Rows: K2, purl to last 2 sts, wyif SL2(p).

> **SL2(k)-K1-P2sso:** (Double Decrease) - Slip 2 sts together knitwise, Knit 1 stitch, Pass 2 slipped sts over.

Row 7: K4, *YO, SL2(k)-K1-P2sso, YO, K3; repeat from * to last 7 sts, YO, SL2(k)-K1-P2sso, YO, K2, wyif SL2(p).

Row 9: K3, *K2tog, YO, K1, YO, SSK, K1; repeat from* to last 2 sts, wyif SL2(p).

Row 11: K2, K2tog, *YO, K3, YO, SL2(k)-K1-P2sso; repeat from * to last 7 sts, YO, K3, YO, SSK, wyif SL2(p).

Row 12: As Row 2.

Repeat 12 rows of FALLING LEAVES PATTERN until sweater measures - *Long length:* 22 (22.5, 23, 23, 24.5, 25)"/56 (57, 58.5, 58.5, 62, 63.5) cm *OR Short length:* 17 (18, 19, 19, 20, 21)"/43 (46, 48, 48, 51, 53.5) cm measuring from bottom of collar to needle OR 2"/5 cm less than desired length, ending after a Row 6 or 12.

Double Ridge:

Change to smaller circular needle (30"/80 cm long).

Row 1: (RS) K2, purl to last 2 sts, wyif SL2(p).

Row 2: Knit to last 2 sts, wyif SL2(p).

Row 3: K3, *YO, SSK, K1, K2tog, YO, K1; repeat from * to last 2 sts, wyif SL2(p).

Row 4: K2, purl to last 2 sts, wyif SL2(p).

Row 5: K2, purl to last 2 sts, wyif SL2(p).

In next row, adjust number of stitches for lace pattern to follow:

Row 6: Knit to last 2 sts, wyif SL2(p), increasing (+) or decreasing (-) sts evenly across the row according to your size below:

Size 1: + 3 sts	(224 sts)
Size 2: + 5 sts	(244 sts)
Size 3: - 7 sts	(244 sts)
Size 4: - 5 sts	(264 sts)
Size 5: - 3 sts	(284 sts)
Size 6: - 1 st	(304 sts)

CORONA BORDER

Tip: In the first row below I suggest placing a marker between each repeat of the pattern. It will be easier to keep track of sts and to notice if there is an error. The stitch count changes throughout the pattern. Note that the first and last 2 sts of every row are the I-Cord edge.

Row 1: (RS) K2, *K10, [YO] twice, K10, place marker; repeat from * to last 2 sts, wyif SL2(p).

Row 2: (WS) K2, *K3, P7, make 5 new sts out of the double YO loop by working [K1, P1, K1, P1, K1] into this loop, P7, K3; repeat from * to last 2 sts, wyif SL2(p).

Row 3: K2, *K2, SSK, K17, K2tog, K2; repeat from * to last 2 sts, wyif SL2(p).

Row 4: K2, *K3, P17, K3; repeat from * to last 2 sts, wyif SL2(p).

Row 5: K2, *K2, SSK, K5, [YO, K1] 5 times, YO, K5, K2tog, K2; repeat from * to last 2 sts, wyif SL2(p),

Row 6: K2, *K3, P5, K11, P5, K3; repeat from * to last 2 sts, wyif SL2(p).

Row 7: K2, *K2, SSK, K19, K2tog, K2; repeat from * to last 2 sts, wyif SL2(p).

Row 8: K2, *K3, P4, K11, P4, K3; repeat from * to last 2 sts, wyif SL2(p).

Row 9: K2, *K2, SSK, K2, [SSK, YO] 3 times, K1, [YO, K2tog] 3 times, K2, K2tog, K2; repeat from * to last 2 sts, wyif SL2(p).

Row 10: K2, *K3, P3, K11, P3, K3; repeat from * to last 2 sts, wyif SL2(p).

Row 11: K2, *K2, SSK, K15, K2tog, K2; repeat from * to last 2 sts, wyif SL2(p).

Row 12: K2, *K3, P2, K11, P2, K3; repeat from * to last 2 sts, wyif SL2(p).

Row 13: K2, *K2, [SSK] twice, [YO, SSK] twice, YO, K1, [YO, K2tog] 3 times, K4; repeat from * to last 2 sts, wyif SL2(p). - 224 (244, 244, 264, 284, 304) sts

Row 14: SSK, knit to last 2 sts, K2tog.

With larger needle, **Cast Off** knitways.

SLEEVES

The sleeves are a little longer than usual to give the cuff a bit of a ruffle effect. However, they can be adjusted to your preferred length. Sleeves are worked 'in the round'.

Set-Up Round: *With shorter circular needle,* starting at the centre of the cast on sts at underarm of Body, attach yarn and from underarm sts, pick up and knit 4 (6, 6, 6, 7, 7) sts, pick up one extra st to close the gap, knit around the 76 (80, 84, 88, 92, 96) sleeve sts, pick up and knit one extra st to close the gap, pick up and knit 3 (5, 5, 5, 6, 6) sts from the cast on sts at underarm. Join in the round and place a marker. - 85 (93, 97, 101, 107, 111) sts.

Next Round: K3 (5, 5, 5, 6, 6) sts, K2tog, knit around sleeve sts to 4 (6, 6, 6, 7, 7) sts from end of round, SSK, knit to end of round. - 83 (91, 95, 99, 105, 109) sts.

Sleeve Decreases:

Knit 5 (5, 4, 4, 3, 3) rounds even.

Decrease Round: K1, K2tog, knit to 2 sts before marker, SSK.

Repeat last 6 (6, 5, 5, 4, 4) rounds until sleeves are 17"/43 cm or approximately 2"/5 cm less than desired length. Do Not decrease to less than 49 sts. If necessary, continue to knit every round on 49 sts to desired length.

Double Ridge: (in the round)

Next Round: Knit, decreasing evenly to 49 sts if necessary.

Change to smaller circular needle (16"/40 cm long) or double pointed needles:

Round 1: Purl.

Round 2: Purl.

Round 3: K1, *YO, SSK, K1, K2tog,YO, K1; repeat from * to end of round.

Round 4: Knit.

Rounds 5 and 6: Purl.

Round 7: M1, K2, M1, work [K5, M1] to last 2 sts, K2. (60 sts)

CORONA BORDER (In the round)

Tip: *I suggest placing a stitch marker between each pattern repeat to make it easier to keep track of the pattern or if using double pointed needles put one stitch repeat on each needle.*

Note: *Stitch count changes throughout pattern.*

Round 1: *K10, [YO] twice, K10; repeat from * to end of round.

Round 2: *P3, K7, make 5 new sts out of the double loop by working [K1, P1, K1, P1, K1] into this loop, K7, P3; repeat from * to end of round.

Round 3: *K2, SSK, K17, K2tog, K2; repeat from * to end of round.

Round 4: *P3, K17, P3; repeat from * to end of round.

Round 5: *K2, SSK, K5, [YO, K1] 5 times, YO, K5, K2tog, K2; repeat from * to end of round.

Round 6: *P3, K5, P11, K5, P3; repeat from * to end of round.

Round 7: *K2, SSK, K19, K2tog, K2; repeat from * to end of round.

Round 8: *P3, K4, P11, K4, P3; repeat from * to end of round.

Round 9: *K2, SSK, K2, [SSK, YO] 3 times, K1, [YO, K2tog] 3 times, K2, K2tog, K2; repeat from * to end of round.

Round 10: *P3, K3, P11, K3, P3; repeat from * to end of round.

Round 11: *K2, SSK, K15, K2tog, K2; repeat from * to end of round.

Round 12: *P3, K2, P11, K2, P3; repeat from * to end of round.

Round 13: *K2 , [SSK] twice, [YO, SSK] twice, YO, K1, [YO, K2tog] 3 times, K4; repeat from * to end of round. (60 sts)

Round 14: Purl.

With larger needle, **Cast Off** knitwise.

FINISHING

Weave in all ends. Sew on Buttons.

The Sarah continued from page 78.

SIZES 48 (50½, 53½)"/122 (128.5, 136) cm ONLY

SHORT ROW SHAPING FOR V-NECK

Short Rows are used to shape the V-neck of the cardigan. They are so named because you only work part way across the row, then turn, leaving the rest of the sts in the row unworked on the needle. The short rows chosen for this project give a smooth angle to the side of the V-neck. The short rows are worked below:

Increase SHORT Row 1: (RS of body of cardigan) K2, P1, K1, knit to one stitch before the Marker, M1, K1, slip Marker, K1, M1, K3, P1, K3, M1, K1, slip Marker, K1, M1, K8, work [P1, K3] 6 times, P1, K8, M1, K1, slip Marker, K1, M1, K3, P1, K3, M1, K1, slip Marker, K1, M1, K1, *SSK, K1, Turn.*

Wrong side SHORT Row 2: SL1, purl to first Marker, slip Marker, P5, K1, P5, slip Marker, P10, work [K1, P3] 6 times, K1, P10, slip Marker, P5, K1, P5, slip Marker, P2, *P2tog, P1, Turn.*

Increase SHORT Row 3: (RS) SL1, Knit to one stitch before the Marker, M1, K1, slip Marker, K1, M1, work [P1, K3] twice, P1, M1, K1, slip Marker, K1, M1, K9, work [P1, K3] 6 times, P1, K9, M1, K1, slip Marker, K1, M1, work [P1, K3] twice, P1, M1, K1, slip Marker, K1, M1, knit to one stitch before the gap, *SSK, K1, Turn.*

Wrong side SHORT Row 4: SL1, purl to first Marker, slip Marker, P2, work [K1, P3] twice, K1, P2, slip Marker, P11, work [K1, P3] 6 times, K1, P11, slip Marker, P2, work [K1, P3] twice, K1, P2, slip Marker, purl to one stitch before the gap, *P2tog, P1, Turn.*

Increase SHORT Row 5: (RS) SL1, knit to one stitch before the Marker, M1, K1, slip Marker, K1, M1, K1, work [P1, K3] twice,

P1, K1, M1, K1, slip Marker, K1, M1, K10, work [P1, K3] 6 times, P1, K10, M1, K1, slip Marker, K1, M1, K1, work [P1, K3] twice, P1, K1, M1, K1, slip Marker, K1, M1, knit to one stitch before the gap, *SSK, K1, Turn.*

Wrong side SHORT Row 6: SL1, purl to first Marker, slip Marker, P3, work [K1, P3] 3 times, slip Marker, P12, work [K1, P3] 6 times, K1, P12, slip Marker, P3, work [K1, P3] 3 times, slip Marker, purl to one stitch before the gap, *P2tog, P1, Turn.*

The 25 stitch centre ribbed panel is now well established on the Back.

Increase SHORT Row 7: (RS) SL1, knit to one stitch before the Marker, M1, K1, slip Marker, K1, M1, K2, work [P1, K3] 2 times, P1, K2, M1, K1, slip Marker, K1, M1, knit to centre panel, work rib panel, knit to one stitch before the Marker, M1, K1, slip Marker, K1, M1, K2, work [P1, K3] 2 times, P1, K2, M1, K1, slip Marker, K1, M1, knit to one stitch before the gap, *SSK, K1, Turn.*

Wrong side SHORT Row 8: SL1, purl to first Marker, slip Marker, P4, work [K1, P3] 3 times, P1, slip Marker, purl to centre panel, work rib panel, purl to next Marker, slip Marker, P4, work [K1, P3] 3 times, P1, slip Marker, purl to one stitch before the gap, *P2tog, P1, Turn.*

Increase SHORT Row 9: (RS) SL1, knit to one stitch before the Marker, M1, K1, slip Marker, K1, M1, K3, work [P1, K3] 3 times, M1, K1, slip Marker, K1, M1, knit to centre panel, work rib panel, knit to one stitch before the Marker, M1, K1, slip Marker, K1, M1, K3, work [P1, K3] 3 times, M1, K1, slip Marker, K1, M1, knit to one stitch before the gap, *SSK, K1, Turn.*

Wrong side SHORT Row 10: SL1, purl to first Marker, slip Marker, P5, work [K1, P3] 3 times, P2, slip Marker, purl to centre panel, work rib panel, purl to next Marker, slip Marker, P5, work [K1, P3] 3 times, P2, slip Marker, purl to one stitch before the gap, *P2tog, P1, Turn.*

Increase SHORT Row 11: (RS) SL1, knit to one stitch before the Marker, M1, K1, slip Marker, K1, M1, work [P1, K3] 4 times, P1, M1, K1, slip Marker, K1, M1, knit to centre panel, work rib panel, knit to one stitch before the Marker, M1, K1, slip Marker K1, M1, work [P1, K3] 4 times, P1, M1, K1, slip Marker, K1, M1, knit to one stitch before the gap, *SSK, K1, Turn.*

Wrong side SHORT Row 12: SL1, purl to first Marker, slip Marker, P2, work [K1, P3] 4 times, K1, P2, slip Marker, purl to centre panel, work rib panel, purl to next Marker, slip Marker, P2, work [K1, P3] 4 times, K1, P2, slip Marker, purl to one stitch before the gap, *P2tog, P1, Turn.*

Increase SHORT Row 13: (RS) SL1, knit to one stitch before the Marker, M1, K1, slip Marker, K1, M1, K1, work [P1, K3] 4 times, P1, K1, M1, K1, slip Marker, K1, M1, knit to centre panel, work rib panel, knit to one stitch before the Marker, M1, K1, slip Marker, K1, M1, K1, work [P1, K3] 4 times, P1, K1, M1, K1, slip Marker, K1, M1, knit to one stitch before the gap, *SSK, K1, Turn.*

Wrong side SHORT Row 14: SL1, purl to first Marker, slip Marker, P3, work [K1, P3] 5 times, slip Marker, purl to centre panel, work rib panel, purl to next Marker, slip Marker, P3, work [K1, P3] 5 times, slip Marker, purl to one stitch before the gap, *P2tog, P1, Turn.*

Increase SHORT Row 15: (RS) SL1, knit to one stitch before the Marker, M1, K1, slip Marker, K1, M1, K2, work [P1, K3] 4 times, P1, K2, M1, K1, slip Marker, K1, M1, knit to centre panel, work rib panel, knit to one stitch before the Marker, M1, K1, slip Marker, K1, M1, K2, work [P1, K3] 4 times, P1, K2, M1, K1, slip Marker, K1, M1, knit to one stitch before the gap, *SSK, K1, Turn.*

Wrong side SHORT Row 16: SL1, purl to first Marker, slip Marker, P4, work [K1, P3] 5 times, P1, slip Marker, purl to centre panel, work rib panel, purl to next Marker, slip Marker, P4, work [K1, P3] 5 times, P1, slip Marker, purl to one stitch before the gap, *P2tog, P1, Turn.*

Increase SHORT Row 17: (RS) SL1, knit to one stitch before the Marker, M1, K1, slip Marker, K1, M1, K3, work [P1, K3] 5 times, M1, K1, slip Marker, K1, M1, knit to centre panel, work rib panel, knit to one stitch before the Marker, M1, K1, slip Marker, K1, M1, K3, work [P1, K3] 5 times, M1, K1, slip Marker, K1, M1, knit to one stitch before the gap, *SSK, K1, Turn.*

Wrong side SHORT Row 18: SL1, purl to first Marker, slip Marker, P5, work [K1, P3] 5 times, P2, slip Marker, P18, work [K1, P3] 6 times, K1, purl to next Marker, slip Marker, P5, work [K1, P3] 5 times, P2, slip Marker, purl to one stitch before the gap, *P2tog, P1, Turn.*

The 25 stitch ribbed panel is now established on both sleeves.

Increase SHORT Row 19: (RS) SL1, knit to one stitch before the Marker, M1, K1, slip Marker, K1, M1, work [P1, K3] 6 times, P1, M1, K1, slip Marker, K1, M1, knit to centre panel, work rib panel, knit to one stitch before the Marker, M1, K1, slip Marker, K1, M1, work [P1, K3] 6 times, P1, M1, K1, slip Marker, K1, M1, knit to one stitch before the gap, *SSK, K1, Turn.*

Wrong side SHORT Row 20: SL1, purl to first Marker, slip Marker, P2, work [K1, P3] 6 times, K1, P2, slip Marker, purl to centre panel, work rib panel, purl to next Marker, slip Marker, P2, work [K1, P3] 6 times, K1, P2, slip Marker, purl to one stitch before the gap, *P2tog, P1, Turn.*

You have now established the 25 stitch ribbed panel at the centre of each sleeve

and the centre Back of the cardigan.
Continue with the ALL SIZES instructions for remaining SHORT rows.

ALL SIZES

Next Increase SHORT Row: (RS) SL1, knit to one stitch before the Marker, M1, K1, slip Marker, *K1, M1, knit to centre panel, work rib panel, knit to one stitch before the Marker, M1, K1, slip Marker; repeat from * twice more, K1, M1, knit to one stitch before the gap, *SSK, K1, Turn.*

Next Wrong side SHORT Row: SL1, purl to first Marker, slip Marker, *purl to centre panel, work rib panel, purl to next Marker, slip Marker; repeat from * twice more, purl to one stitch before the gap, *P2tog, P1, Turn.*

Repeat the last 2 SHORT Rows until there are 5 sts left unworked on the left needle at the end of each of the last two rows. (4 zipper band sts plus one stitch)

Last Increase SHORT Row: (RS) SL1, knit to one stitch before the Marker, M1, K1, slip Marker, K1, M1, knit to centre panel, work rib panel, knit to one stitch before the next Marker, M1, K1, slip Marker; repeat from * twice more, K1, M1, knit to one stitch before the gap, SSK, (band) K1, P1, K1, wyif SL1(p).

Last Wrong Side SHORT Row: K2, P1, K1 (band), purl to first Marker, slip Marker, *purl to centre panel, work rib panel, purl to next Marker, slip Marker; repeat from * twice more, purl to one stitch before the gap, P2tog, (band) K1, P1, K1, wyif SL1(p).

Short Row Shaping is complete!

CONTINUE WITH YOKE

Note: All rows will now be worked across all sts on the needle. The first and last 4 sts of each row are the zipper band sts.

Increase Row 1: (RS) K2, P1, K1 (band), knit to one stitch before the Marker, M1, K1, slip Marker, *K1, M1, knit to centre panel, work rib panel, knit to one stitch before the next Marker, K1, M1, slip Marker; repeat from * twice more, knit to last 4 sts, (band) K1, P1, K1, wyif SL1(p).

Straight Row 2: K2, P1, K1, purl to Marker, slip Marker, *purl to centre panel, work rib panel, purl to next Marker, slip Marker; repeat from * twice more, purl to last 4 sts, (band) K1, P1, K1, wyif SL1(p).

Repeat Rows 1 & 2 as above until 359 (375, 391, 427, 451, 475) sts on needle.

Reality Check: Number of stitches between markers: Both Fronts have 53 (55, 57, 63, 66, 69) sts, both sleeves have 77 (81, 85, 89, 95, 101) sts, Back has 99 (103, 107, 123, 129, 135) sts.

Work 6 (6, 6, 4, 4, 4) rows even with no further increasing, continuing the Front zipper bands as established.

Divide for Sleeves and Body: With right side facing, work the 4 zipper band sts as set, knit to first Marker, remove the Marker, place next 77 (81, 85, 89, 95, 101) sts of the sleeve on spare yarn, remove the next Marker, Cast On 9 (11, 13, 9, 11, 11) sts for underarm, knit to centre back ribbed pattern, work rib panel as set, knit to the next Marker, remove Marker, place next 77 (81, 85, 89, 95, 101) sts of the sleeve on spare yarn, remove Marker, Cast On 9 (11, 13, 9, 11, 11) sts for underarm, knit to last 4 sts, work zipper band as established. - 223 (235, 247, 267, 283, 295) sts on circular needle for BODY.

Next Row: (WS) Work 4 zipper band sts as set, purl to the centre Back panel, work rib panel as set, purl to last 4 sts, work zipper band as established.

BODY

Note: In the next 2 rows 4 markers will be placed to mark the side seam sts in order to place decreases for the waist.

Set-Up Row: (RS) Work 4 sts of zipper band as set, K53 (56, 59, 63, 67, 70), place side seam Marker, K1, place side seam Marker, knit to centre panel, work rib panel, knit to last 4 sts, work zipper band as set.

Set-Up Row: Work 4 sts of zipper band, P53 (56, 59, 63, 67, 70), place side seam Marker, K1, place side seam Marker, purl to the centre panel, work rib panel, purl to the last 4 sts, work zipper band.

Row 1: (RS) Work 4 sts of zipper band as set, knit to centre panel, work rib panel, knit to last 4 sts, work zipper band.

Row 2: Work 4 sts of zipper band, purl to the centre panel, work rib panel, purl to the last 4 sts, work zipper band.

Rows 3 - 6: Repeat Rows 1 & 2, twice more.

Row 7: Work 4 sts of zipper band, knit to 2 sts before the first Marker, K2tog, slip Marker, K1, slip Marker, SSK, work in patterns as set to 2 sts before next Marker, K2tog, slip Marker, K1, slip Marker, SSK, knit to last 4 sts, work zipper band.

Row 8: Repeat Row 2.

Repeat last 8 rows 2 (1, 2, 1, 2, 2) times more. Remove markers when working the last repeat of Row 8. - 211 (227, 235, 259, 271, 283) sts.

Continue working Rows 1 & 2 ONLY without further decreases until work from centre back of the base of the collar to the needle measures 14½ (14½, 15, 15, 15, 15½)"/37 (37, 38, 38, 38, 39) cm, ending after a WS row. The sweater should come to approximately 2"/5 cm above the recipient's waist. You can lengthen or shorten the sweater at this point.

Work CABLE TWIST PATTERN in the centre Back panel:

Row 1: (RS) Work 4 sts of zipper band, knit to centre Back panel, work Row 1 of CABLE TWIST PATTERN, knit to last 4 sts, work zipper band.

CABLE TWIST PATTERN (25 STS)

Row 1: (RS) P1, work [K3, P1] twice, C7B, work [P1, K3] twice, P1.

Row 2 and every alternate round: (WS) Work [K1, P3] 6 times, K1.

Row 3: (RS) Work [P1, K3] 6 times, P1.

Row 5: P1, K3, P1, work [C7F, P1] twice, K3, P1.

Row 7: Repeat Row 3.

Row 9: P1, work [C7B, P1] 3 times.

Row 11: Repeat Row 3.

Row 13: P1, K3, P1, work [C7F, P1] twice, K3, P1.

Row 15: Repeat Row 3.

Row 17: (RS) P1, work [K3, P1] twice, C7B, work [P1, K3] twice, P1.

Row 18: (WS) Work [K1, P3] 6 times, K1.

C7B: (Cable 7 Back) Slip next 4 sts onto cable needle and hold at back of work, knit next 3 sts on left-hand needle, slip purl st from cable needle onto left-hand needle and purl it, then knit 3 sts from cable needle.

C7F: (Cable 7 Front) Slip next 4 sts onto cable needle and hold at front of work, knit next 3 sts on left-hand needle, slip purl st from cable needle onto left-hand needle and purl it, then knit 3 sts from cable needle.

Row 2: Work 4 sts of zipper band, purl to centre Back panel, work Row 2 of CABLE TWIST PATTERN, purl to last 4 sts, work zipper band.

Row 3: (RS) Work 4 sts of zipper band, knit to centre Back panel, work next row of CABLE TWIST PATTERN, knit to last 4 sts, work zipper band.

Row 4: Work 4 sts of zipper band, purl to centre Back panel, work next row of CABLE TWIST PATTERN, purl to last 4 sts, work zipper band.

Repeat last Rows 3 & 4, 7 times more to complete the CABLE TWIST PATTERN.

RIBBED BAND

Set-Up Row 1: (RS) Work 4 sts of zipper band as set, knit to centre Back panel

decreasing 1 st, work rib panel as [P1, K3] 6 times, P1, knit to last 4 sts decreasing 1 st, work zipper band as set.   - 209 (225, 233, 257, 269, 281) sts.

Row 2: (WS) Work 4 sts of zipper band as set, work [K1, P3] to last 5 sts, K1, work 4 sts of zipper band as established.

Row 3: (RS) Work 4 sts of zipper band as set, [P1, K3] to last 5 sts, P1, work 4 sts of zipper band as set.

Row 4: (WS) Work 4 sts of zipper band as set, work [K1, P3] to last 5 sts, K1, work 4 sts of zipper band as established.

Repeat Rows 3 and 4 until ribbed band measures 5"/13 cm, ending after a WS row.

Cast Off while purling.

SLEEVES (WORKED IN THE ROUND)

Sleeve Set-Up Round 1: *With the smaller circular needle (16"/40 cm long),* starting at the centre of underarm cast on sts, attach yarn and pick up and knit 5 (6, 7, 5, 6, 6) sts from underarm cast on sts, pick up one extra st to close gap, knit to centre panel, work rib panel, knit to the end of sleeve sts, pick up and knit one extra st to close gap, pick up and knit 4 (5, 6, 4, 5, 5), join in the round and place Marker. - 88 (94, 100, 100, 108, 114) sts.

Set-Up Round 2: K4 (5, 6, 4, 5, 5), K2tog, knit to centre panel, work rib panel, knit to 5 (6, 7, 5, 6, 6) sts before the Marker, SSK, knit to Marker. - 86 (92, 98, 98, 106, 112) sts.

Sleeve Decreases:

Change to double pointed needles when the number of stitches require it.

Work 5 (5, 4, 4, 3, 3) Rounds: Knit to centre panel, work rib panel, knit to end of round.

Next (Decrease) Round: K1, SSK, knit to centre panel, work rib panel, knit to last 2 sts, K2tog.

Repeat last 6 (6, 5, 5, 4, 4) rounds until sleeve is approximately 14"/36 cm long OR 5"/13 cm short of desired sleeve length. (This sleeve is designed to extend past the wrist over the hand about 1½"/4 cm - 2"/5 cm.) Do not decrease to less than 52 (52, 56, 56, 56) sts.

Work the TWIST CABLE PATTERN below over the 25 stitch centre ribbed pattern AT THE SAME TIME continue to repeat last 6 (6, 5, 5, 4, 4) rounds of Sleeve Decrease if

necessary until you have 52 (52, 56, 56, 56, 56) sts. Continue even on 52 (52, 56, 56, 56, 56) sts to finish the Twisted Cable Pattern.

TWIST CABLE PATTERN FOR SLEEVE (WORKED OVER THE 25 STS OF CENTRE RIB PANEL)

Round 1: P1, work [K3, P1] twice, C7B, work [P1, K3] twice, P1.

Round 2 and every alternate round: Work [P1, K3] 6 times, P1.

Round 3: Work [P1, K3] 6 times, P1.

Round 5: P1, K3, P1, work [C7F, P1] twice, K3, P1.

Round 7: Repeat Round 3.

Round 9: P1, work [C7B, P1] 3 times.

Round 11: Repeat Round 3.

Round 13: P1, K3, P1, work [C7F, P1] twice, K3, P1.

Round 15: Repeat Round 3.

Round 17: P1, work [K3, P1] twice, C7B, work [P1, K3)] twice, P1.

C7B: (Cable 7 Back) Slip next 4 sts onto cable needle and hold at back of work, knit next 3 sts on left-hand needle, slip purl st from cable needle onto left-hand needle and purl it, then knit 3 sts from cable needle.

C7F: (Cable 7 Front) Slip next 4 sts onto cable needle and hold at front of work, knit next 3 sts on left-hand needle, slip purl st from cable needle onto left-hand needle and purl it, then knit 3 sts from cable needle.

CUFF

Decrease Round: Using the 2 side knit sections decrease evenly to 52 (52, 56, 56, 56) sts if necessary as you work: knit to centre panel, work [P1, K3] 6 times, P1, knit to end of round, remove marker.

In the next round the ribbing for the cuff is set up. The rib pattern will begin with the centre rib panel and continue around the cuff and then back to the centre panel where the rib pattern should match up.

Set-Up Round: Knit to the beginning edge of centre panel, begin working [P1, K3] across the centre panel and continue around the whole cuff and back to the beginning edge of the centre panel. (The ribbed cuff is now established to work into the centre panel.)

Work [P1, K3] rib as set until cuff measures 3"/7.5 cm or desired length.

Cast Off purlwise. **Note:** I recommend starting the Cast Off on the underside of

the cuff at approximately the underarm seam line.

FINISHING

Work in yarn ends, sew in the zipper and enjoy your cardigan!

ABBREVIATIONS & TERMS

IT'S A BIG WORLD OUT THERE

There are certain differences in word usage in Canada, the United States, Europe, Australia, New Zealand and every other knitting-mad country.

Some examples include spelling (colour versus color), which are pretty easy to work out and other differences in actual words (in Canada we use Cast Off, but Bind Off is more usual in the U.S.) and there are wildly different needle sizes used.

So, to help out, the section Terms Used covers terminology used in the patterns and an explanation of differences.

MEASUREMENTS

We have included measurements in both imperial (inches) and metric (centimeters) in our patterns, along with yards and meters for yarn requirements.

Yarn weights are generally indicated in grams (i.e. 50g) but for clarification, a 100 gram ball is approximately 3 1/2 oz. One ounce equals 28.35 grams.

Additionally, needle sizes are indicated in both metric (ie 4.0mm) and US sizes (US6).

We think that covers it!

TERMS USED & ABBREVIATIONS

- **(curved brackets)** are used to indicate different instructions for different sizes. The smallest size is in front of the bracket and the larger sizes are inside the brackets. ie. 80 (88, 94) sts.
  Curved brackets may also be used to show that the instructions inside the brackets should be worked as a unit.

- **[square brackets]** indicate that whatever is inside the brackets should be worked as a unit and worked the number of times indicated. If the instructions read: [K4, P4] twice, you should: K4, P4, K4, P4, ...

- **Aran or heavy worsted weight:** yarn with a gauge of 18 sts = 4"/10 cm

- **As established** or **as set** means to continue to work the stitch, cable or colour pattern as you have previously been instructed. Simply carry on with the pattern.

- **Backward Loop:** Increase one stitch, see page 102.

- **C7B:** (Cable 7 Back) Slip next 4 sts onto cable needle and hold at back of work, knit next 3 sts on left-hand needle, slip purl st from cable needle onto left-hand needle and purl it, then knit 3 sts from cable needle.

- **C7F:** (Cable 7 Front) Slip next 4 sts onto cable needle and hold at front of work, knit next 3 sts on left-hand needle, slip purl st from cable needle onto left-hand needle and purl it, then knit 3 sts from cable needle.

- **Cast Off** is also known as bind-off and is the process of finishing the edge of a bottom edging or sleeve cuff.

- **CC:** Contrast Colour.

- **DK (double knitting weight):** yarn with gauge of 22 sts = 4"/10 cm.

- **End with a wrong side row** means complete the instructions by working a wrong side row.

- **Fair Isle** is a repeating pattern with two or more colours, where all the colours of yarn are "carried" along the row or round where the pattern is used.

- **Garter Stitch:** When *Knitting Flat* you knit every row. When *Knitting in the Round* it is a two round sequence: knit one round and purl the next round.

- **Gauge or Tension:** The number of stitches over 1 or 4 inches (2.5 cm or 10 cm) of knitting obtained with a specific needle size, generally measured over stocking stitch unless otherwise indicated.

A gauge over 4"/10 cm.
> 22 sts = 4"/10 cm on
> 4.0mm/US6 needles
> A gauge over 1"/2.5 cm.
> 5.5 sts = 1"/2.5 cm on
> 4.0mm/US6 needles

It is important to know the recommended tension when you wish to substitute yarns. Not all yarns with the same ball band tension will be totally interchangeable as different fibre content can affect how the yarn works up, but it is a good starting point.

- **INC-1:** Increase one stitch, see page 102.

- **K2tog:** Knit two sts together (right slanting decrease).

- **Kfb:** Increase of 1 stitch also known as knitting into the front and back of a stitch. Knit into the front of the next stitch as usual and without taking the stitch off the left needle, then knit into the back of the same stitch.

- **Left Front/Right Front:** means the left or right side of the front of the sweater as if you were wearing the garment.

- **M1:** Make one stitch. See Increases on page 102.

- **Markers** (stitch markers). A marker is a device (a piece of yarn tied in a circle, a coloured plastic or rubber ring, etc.) which you put on your needle to indicate a certain point in your knitting, such as the beginning of a round or the beginning or end of a panel of textured sts, cable or colour pattern.

- **MC:** Main Colour.

- **ML1:** Make one Loop. See page 60.

- **Open M1:** Make one stitch. See Increases on page 102.

- **P2tog:** Purl two sts together.

- **Pick up and knit:** using the right-hand needle, insert the needle through an edge stitch, for example, and loop the yarn around your needle. Complete the stitch by bringing the loop through to the right side. This makes a stitch on the right-hand needle. This is often used to continue knitting in a different direction without working separate pieces and sewing them together.

- **Place marker** and **Slip marker:** Placing a marker means to put the marker onto the right-hand needle. On the next round or row, work to a marker and "slip it" or transfer it from the left-hand needle.

- **Right Side (RS)** is the public side or the side that will be seen when sweater is worn. **Wrong Side (WS)** is the side not shown to the public, and is next to your body.

- **SL1:** Slip one stitch. Transfer the stitch from the left-hand needle to the right-hand needle without working the stitch. Unless instructed otherwise, the stitch is slipped as if to purl (insert your right-hand needle tip as if you are about to purl the stitch and slip it off the left-hand needle).

- **Shapeline:** The shapelines are the two knit stitches separating each pair of raglan increases which create the distinctive diagonal line of the raglan yoke. Each shapeline has a marker set between these two stitches.

- **SL2(k)-K1-P2sso:** (Double Decrease) - Slip 2 sts together knitwise, Knit 1 stitch, Pass 2 slipped sts over.

- **SSK:** Slip, slip, knit (left leaning decrease). Slip one stitch as if to knit, slip next stitch as if to knit, insert the left needle into the front of the two slipped sts, from left to right, and knit them together.

- **Stocking (stockinette) stitch.** It is a two row sequence: knit one row and purl one row. When *Knitting in the Round* knit every round.

- **wyif SL2(p)** - with yarn in front, slip 2 sts purlwise

- **YO (Yarn over)** is a method for making an increase and creating a deliberate, decorative hole in the knitting. Bring wool under the right needle and forward to the front of your work, swing the wool over the right needle to the back of your work. The resulting loop is worked as a stitch in the next row or round.

- **Yardage:** The length of yarn contained in a ball or skein. The pattern will indicate the number of balls used and the yardage of each ball. You will need to purchase the correct total amount of yards or meters to complete the garment. If a pattern calls for 50g of yarn, this is not an accurate representation of the quantity needed. Cotton, for example, is heavier than wool and 50g of cotton may not go as far as 50g of wool. The short form for yardage is yds.

INCREASES

There are a number of methods for increasing stitches. In the Basic DK and Basic Aran patterns you can choose any of the following increases. In the Variations the designer will give specific instructions in order to obtain a specific result. Check the pattern carefully.

Backward loop increase: Make an increase by putting a backward loop on the right-hand needle. It will be worked as a stitch in the next round.

Also used to Cast On underarm stitches.

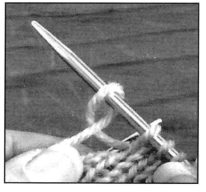

A backward loop prior to tightening it on the needle.

M1: Make one stitch (no holes). With the left-hand needle lift the running thread between the stitch just worked and the next stitch, from front to back, and knit into the back of the resulting loop.

To be symmetrical, on the other side of the shapeline, with left-hand needle lift the running thread from back to front, and knit the resulting loop. *(Note: This one is tighter to knit into.)*

(Open) M1: (with holes) Insert right-hand needle under the running thread between the stitch just worked and next stitch without lifting or twisting it, wrap yarn around needle and bring to the front.

YO: Yarn Over: Yarn over to make a hole (eyelet) and increase one stitch. Bring wool under the right needle and forward to the front of your work, swing the wool over the right needle to the back of your work, ready to work the next stitch.

The wool has been brought under the right needle and forward to the front of the work , then over the needle to the back in preparation to knit the next stitch.

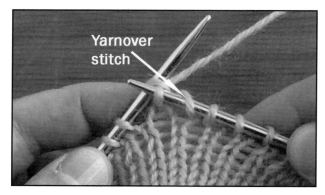

The next stitch being worked.

TECHNICAL BITS

EQUIPMENT

As any good craftsperson knows, you need good tools to do your job right. Luckily, for this craft you don't need to run out and buy a circular saw for a couple hundred dollars! However, you should have a good range of knitting needles appropriate for the job.

You'll need:

- Circular needles;
- Sets of double pointed needles; and
- A cable needle, if you are doing a cable design
- markers;
- Tapestry needle or blunt sewing-up needle.

CIRCULAR NEEDLES

Circular needles come in many varieties. You can get them in plastic, steel, nickel and bamboo as a minimum. Plastic and bamboo needles are good if you are working with a slippery yarn (cotton, some wools, mohair etc), and they are also light and warm. Metal needles are great for speed as they slide your yarn along with no hesitation. Try out different needles with different yarn to see what you like.

Circular needles also come in varying lengths. Commonly they are:

40 cm / 16 inches
60 cm / 24 inches
80 cm / 36 inches
100 cm / 40 inches

It is important to carefully check the join where the needle tips are attached to the connecting plastic wire. If the join is rough you will be unhappy working with these needles because they may catch or snag your yarn as you move it back and forth across the join.

When you get new circular needles they will be coiled up in the package. If you try to work with the needles without preparing them first they will, at the very least, be stiff and hard to work with. At their worst, they'll try to coil up your knitting as you work on it, and drive you crazy.

To prepare your needles for comfortable knitting, remove them from the package and place them in really hot tap water. The plastic connecting wire should relax quite a bit and become pliable and relatively straight. Do not store the needle back in the package when finished with it.

DOUBLE POINTED NEEDLES

You will need these for the sleeves worked in the round.

double pointed needles (dpns) are available in sets of four or five needles. We always use five needle sets but this is a matter of personal preference. Whatever number of needles you use, one needle is used to work the stitches while the knit stitches rest on the other needles.

As with circular needles, double pointed needles come in various materials such as wood, bamboo, plastic and various metals. They also come in a range of lengths, from glove sizes which are less than 5 inches, to short needles around 5½ to 6 inches (14 cm to 15 cm), to common lengths of 7-ish inches to 20 inches (18 cm to 51 cm).

GAUGE SWATCH

We do recommend working a gauge swatch. A swatch gives you a sample of your knitting with a particular yarn and needle size.

Work the Swatch:

Since you are going to be knitting one of the cardigans, the majority of the garment is knit flat so you should knit your swatch a flat, knitting on the right side and purling on the wrong side. Adjust the needle as you work until you find the right needle size to obtain the given tension.

With a ruler, count the number of stitches you have over 4"/10 cm of knitting.

If you are getting too few stitches over 4"/10 cm then try a smaller needle size. If you are getting more stitches in the 4"/10 cm than the gauge calls for, then try a larger needle.

You should also treat the swatch to whatever washing method you will be using for the finished garment. If the yarn is a machine washable (superwash) yarn then machine wash the swatch and measure it after it's dry. If it's a hand wash item, take it to the sink and wash by hand for your test.

FINISHING

Sewing on Buttons:

For extra security we suggest the use of shirt buttons sewn on the back of the actual sweater button.

Set a button over the buttonhole on the appropriate side. Using button thread, close the hole as you attach the button. After 2-3 passes of the thread, attach a small shirt button on the wrong side of the button band and sew through both buttons. This adds stability and strength for the buttons.

Zippers:

Baste zipper into place and hand stitch securely. Deb found using a fabic glue (which washes out) to hold the zipper in place, worked very well for her.

OTHER READING

Whether you are an absolute or relative beginner, or an experienced knitter there are always useful and interesting books and reference materials that are worthwhile to look through.

For knitting Top Down:

Knitting from the Top by Barbara G. Walker, Scribner, 1972.

Top Down for Toddlers by Deb & Lynda Gemmell, Cabin Fever, 2004.

Reference books:

Knitting for Dummies by Pam Allen, Hungry Minds, 2002. This is an excellent reference book.

The Complete Idiot's Guide to Knitting and Crocheting by Gail Diven and Cindy Kitchel, Alpha Books, 1999.

The Vogue Reference Book, Pantheon, 1989.

The Principles of Knitting, Methods and Techniques of Hand Knitting by June Hemmons Hiatt, Simon and Schuster, 1988.

The Barbara G. Walker's *A Treasury of Knitting Patterns* collection, Schoolhouse Press.

For knitting in the round:

Any book by Elizabeth Zimmermann! All of these books are published by Schoolhouse Press and can be obtained from the web site: http://www.schoolhousepress.com

Knitting Around, Knitting Without Tears, Knitter's Almanac, Knitting Workshop. All are excellent!

Decorative finishes:

Knitting Beyond the Edge: The Essential Collection of Decorative Finishes by Nicky Epstein, Sixth & Spring Books, 2007.

SUPPLY SOURCES

YARN

Cabin Fever
256 Hughes Road
Orillia, ON L3V 2M4
(800) 671-9112
E-mail: info@cabinfever.ca

(Cotton Tweed DK, Wildridge, Button Up Your Top Down, Top Down for Toddlers, Kids' Knitted Hats, Kids' Knitted Sweaters & More)

Our Cotton Tweed DK, patterns and books are available wholesale or retail. We have a number of other top down patterns and many, many, knit in the round garments for adults and children which you can find at good yarn shops or visit our web site at:

http://www.cabinfever.ca

Arnhild's Knitting Studio
2315 Buchanan Drive
Ames, IA, 50010-4370
(515) 598-4391
http://www.arnhild.com

(Ruma 3 tr. Strikke-garn)

Black Water Abby
(720) 320-1003
http://www.abbeyyarns.com

(Black Water Abbey 2 ply)

Brown Sheep Company, Inc.
100662 County Road 16
Mitchell, Nebraska 69357
(800) 826-9136

(Nature Spun, Lamb's Pride)

Kraemer Yarns
P.O. Box 72
Nazareth, PA, 18064-0072
(800) 759-5601

(Tatamy Tweed, Tatamy Tweed Worsted, Naturally Nazareth)

Lanaknits Designs/Hemp for Knitting
Suite 3B, 320 Vernon Street
Nelson, BC, V1L 2G5, Canada
(888) 301-0011
http://www.lanaknits.com

(allhemp6)

Manos del Uruguay In Canada:
Ashley Yarns
Hamilton , ON L8H 4A1
(866) 919-0995

Manos del Uruguay in the US:
Fairmount Fibers
Address: 915 N. 28th St
Philadelphia, PA 19130
(888) 566-9970

(Manos Cotton Stria)

Needful Yarns
4476 Chesswood Drive Unit 10-11
Toronto, Ontario, Canada M3J 2B9
(866) 800-4700

(Extra Stampato Merino)

S. R. Kertzer
50 Trowers Road,
Woodbridge, ON, L4L 7K6,
(800) 263-2354

(Butterfly Super 10 cotton, Stylecraft Marrakech, SRK Collection Mozart)

SheepStrings

51 Main Street East,
Huntsville, ON P1H 2B8, Canada
(866) 253-8852

(Windermere hand-painted)

SweaterKits

http://www.sweaterkits.com
(877) 232-9415

(CottonLicious)

BUTTONS

Bull's Eye Buttons
PO Box 1416
Chautauqua, NY
(716) 357-2500

All buttons are individually handcrafted of polymer clay. They are machine washable and may be put in the dryer on low. They should not be drycleaned. We recommend laundering your garment turned to the inside. All button designs are copyrighted and done in limited editions.

INDEX

MANLY QUIRKS

First it must be stated that we are quite fond of men. As fathers, husbands, sons, nephews and in any number of other roles from boyfriends to bosses to buddies, we think they're peachy. As sweater-wearers though, it does seem to Deb and me that they often lack a certain adventurous something. But was that impression just our feminine-centric view? Could it be that the sweaters in this book – designed for women – would look equally smart over those broader, manly shoulders?

Clearly, research was called for. I took on the onerous task of approaching men (including complete strangers, I must add) to ask what they like in a cardigan. Young, old, and in-between, I braved the odd looks and odder reactions, all for this oh-so-vital research.

The results? Sadly, this gloriously unscientific cross-border study of North American men revealed that while the men themselves aren't boring, their tastes in sweaters are!

When asked what colours they like for sweaters, the answers covered a very subdued rainbow: brown, black, brown, grey, blue, black, brown, navy. Yes, I sensed the theme too. From this in-depth study, an avant garde colour selection for many men would include a green heather, denim blue, perhaps a subtle fleck or, going really wild, a light blue.

And what, above all else, makes a sweater "manly"? Well, the surprising answer was "a zipper". Yes, a zipper is VERY manly. Older gents were quite happy with buttoned-up cardigans but almost all younger men insisted on zippers. By the way, younger guys never call them "cardigans"; they're "jackets" or "sweaters". Cardigans are for grandpa I gather. I confess I felt quite old at that point.

So now you have it! The answer to the question: What do guys want?

But (yes, another but), with the much younger guys (say 18 – 25) retro is big again. Actually I even had a cool 44 year old mention that. So grandpa cardigans with buttons and pockets are cool. Who knew?

And last but not least, most of the men did not give much thought to the fit of the cardigan, except for the larger guys I talked to (tall and/or big) who seemed most concerned that the sweater not be too tight around and under the arms.

So now you have it, the answer to the question: What do guys want?

So:

* keep the colours muted;
* young = zipper; check on acceptability of buttons;
* pockets seem to be highly individual;
* men tend to wear their sweaters closer to the body than we do so maybe not quite as much overall ease as we might for ourselves (think snug, add 2-3"/5-7.5 cm to the chest measurement for the final sweater size or better yet, measure a much loved sweater);
* sleeves MUST be long enough – err on the long side;
* men also like a hip length sweater, around the top of their pant pockets;
* fit: several "big" guys (tall/large size) wanted the arm depth to be roomy, too tight and they can't move well. Make the Yoke longer by knitting several extra rows even after you have reached the required number of stitches at the bottom of the Yoke.

Top down raglans are ideal for fitting the sweater as you go.

So venture out and get knitting for the guys!

- Lynda

A STORY OF TWO SISTERS

Cabin Fever is the business created by us, sisters Deb and Lynda Gemmell, to feed our knitting habit. From an idea hatched on the deck of our Northern Ontario cabin over several summers, Cabin Fever has grown into the largest independent hand-knitting pattern publisher in Canada.

With Deb as the knitting technical expert and Lynda contributing the business and computer know-how, we launched Cabin Fever in 1997.

We began with a tiny retail shop so "cosy" that we could not have more than one customer and one of us in the place at the same time.

But much as we enjoy working with knitters who happen to be customers, our real passion was not running a retail store. We had a much greater interest in producing and publishing our own designs.

So, Cabin Fever the design company was born. Our first hat pattern was launched in 1998 and is still selling strongly.

During the exercise of writing our first patterns we also developed our own distinctive pattern writing style, which has continued to this day. Our patterns are longer than many, as we like to ensure that you know why you are doing a particular technique, as well as how.

The success of our initial patterns has lead us to concentrate our efforts into the production of new designs. Over time, it also lead us to the decision to broaden our designer base. But it wasn't a decision we made lightly!

Our concern was to ensure that when you pick up a Cabin Fever pattern you can make certain assumptions about the pattern and its structure: you will get a wearable garment with minimal finishing, simplicity in approach, and clear instructions with useful "chat" to keep you company as you progress.

Would we be able to continue to provide this level of service with new designers? Ultimately we decided we could, with care, and Friends of Cabin Fever was born.

We approached our friend Shirley Scott (aka Shirl the Purl) and in 2001 Shirl's first pattern was published. We now have more Canadian designers publishing under the Cabin Fever Friends' umbrella, and you'll find their work showcased in this book.

The making of this book was challenging, exciting and extremely rewarding. We hope you get as much pleasure from it as we have!

DEB GEMMELL

Deb started knitting from the top down when her own children were little tykes, for all the reasons that have kept this technique in her repertoire: easy length adjustment to accommodate growth spurts, knitting that's easy enough for a beginner since children's clothes don't have as many picky fitting issues, and of course no sewing up! Although she respects the time consuming and detailed work involved to sew up the pieces, Deb admits to having wardrobes of unfinished sweaters tucked away in closets due to her personal aversion to what has traditionally come after the knitting is finished.

What can we look forward to from Deb? Her project bag now includes a lot of socks, some more top down projects and recently she's been playing with interesting textured stitch patterns (and renovating her bedroom to provide more stash space).

LYNDA GEMMELL

Although Lynda's travels have taken to her to over 18 countries, now it's more often her patterns for Cabin Fever that get to see the world. Those "What do we want to do?" conversations on the deck with her sister Deb launched Lynda out of the corporate sphere, and into a much more enjoyable career as designer, website wrangler, publisher, and creative entrepreneur. This could explain her fondness for designing hats - she wears so many!

When she's not knitting, thinking about knitting or writing or formatting knitting patterns you might find Lynda pursuing one of her other interests: working at her other business of book development, reading mystery stories in the bathtub, dancing the night away, doting on her nieces and nephews, or spending time on the cross-trainer at the Y.

Deb and Lynda's designs have been published in the Knit Hats!, Knit Baby Heads & Toes!, Knit Christmas Stockings! hard cover series of books, all from Storey Publishing, Donna Kooler's Encyclopedia of Knitting, Leisure Arts, 2004. Deb & Lynda's books include: Top Down for Toddlers, Cabin Fever, 2004, Kids' Knitted Hats, Leisure Arts, 2005, Kids' Knitted Sweaters & More, Leisure Arts, 2006.

FRIENDS OF CABIN FEVER

DANA GIBBONS

We're inspired by Dana — a self-taught knitter who learned during her breaks while working as a nurse in an Infant Intensive Care Unit. Once she mastered stitch formation, she forged ahead. As her patterns (and beautifully-dressed granddaughters) demonstrate, Dana has never looked back.

Among the benefits of top-down knitting, Dana cites the ease of working this method in the places she often knits — while travelling, at sports events, or in waiting rooms — because it's easier to have all the pieces together and row counts correct.

Dana brings her experience as a mother of four to these projects, with practical touches like extra buttons for security, looser neck bands to accommodate kids' heads being larger in proportion to their bodies than adults', and buttonholes on both sides of the garment so it's equally wearable, whether handed down to a girl or boy.

Dana has designs pubished in *Top Down for Toddlers*, by Cabin Fever, *Kids' Knitted Hats* and *Kids' Knitted Sweaters & More*, by Leisure Arts.

KAREN LAWRENCE

Karen's passion for knitting has recently met her desire to create unique and fashionable designs. Forever mixing it up and always in for a challenge, Karen's designs reflect her eye for colour and flair as well as incorporating her playful nature.

Karen's love of yarn, texture and colour is evident in her yarn shop, SheepStrings, located in Huntsville, Ontario. A supporter of the "all-in one" type of knitting, it was a natural fit for Karen to contribute to our new collection.

Whilst life often gets in the way, as she is a mother, wife and business person, Karen admits that the pursuit of texture and colour are her true passions. Karen sites her mother and grandmother as her inspirations to the world of knitting and still recalls the green scarf she knit as her first project. She was the proudest four year old alive and she hasn't stopped since!

Karen has received two nominations for her business endeavours. The YWCA Women of Distinction and the Huntsville Chamber of Commerce New Business of the Year Award. She was featured in the several local newspapers, CBC radio and the Toronto Sun for her Teardrop Scarf Project, a fundraiser for Cancer Recovery and a memorial to her father.

MEGAN LACEY

A knitter from age 8, Megan has been designing her own patterns since 1996. Originally inspired by her grandmother's beautiful handknit sweaters, today Megan finds her ideas in the colours and patterns of nature; the simplicity of moss growing over an unusual shaped rock can be all it takes to spark the idea for a sweater.

When asked what advice she has for knitters, Megan says it's important to get the tension right; if you don't knit to the correct tension, you won't get the right size. She also believes that knitters should buy good quality yarn because, after all the work put into making a sweater, it should be made in something that will last.

Megan knits mostly Nordic styles, and her designs tend to have Fair Isle patterns in them — a seemingly complex technique that Megan makes surprisingly simple to knit.

Megan has designs published in Knitter's Magazine and the *Socks, Socks, Socks* book & *Kids, A Knitters Dozen* by XRX, *Top Down for Toddlers*, by Cabin Fever, *Kids' Knitted Hats* and *Kids' Knitted Sweaters & More*, by Leisure Arts.

BERNICE VOLLICK

Bernice started knitting for her dolls when she was just 7 or 8. From doll clothes she moved to socks - for brothers, father, and finally for a boyfriend who became her life partner. Early in the relationship he endeared himself by respecting the phrase "just wait until I finish this row."

Over the years knitting for her three children, nieces and nephews, and then another young generation, Bernice could not resist the urge to design a few change to patterns, making them her own. The next step was "What pattern? Who needs a pattern?"

With the encouragement of the Cabin Fever sisters and their anti-finishing style, Bernice was drawn into the world of design. Her fresh approach embraces minimal finishing, and also means that not every pattern has to be knit from the bottom up or top down – what's wrong with a little sideways for variety?

Bernice works full time, but looks forward to retirement, and more time for knitting, designing, and more knitting, maybe for great grandchildren some time in the future!

Bernie has designs pubished in *Top Down for Toddlers*, by Cabin Fever, *Kids' Knitted Hats* and *Kids' Knitted Sweaters & More*, by Leisure Arts.

OUR DESIGN PHILOSOPHY

Simply put, we're nuts about knitting, but not about the dreaded sewing-up that has traditionally come after the knitting is done.

So, our overall knitting philosophy is simple. We believe that, within reason, when you finish knitting and have worked that final cast off, you're finished! We don't want to sew seams, or wrestle in sleeves that don't seem to fit into armholes.

We don't like to feel that the knitting is just a small part of creating a finished garment.

We're knitters and we love to knit but neither one of us likes to sew. It just makes us cranky!

We believe that when you are finished the knitting — you're finished the garment!

The majority of our designs are knit in one piece, from the bottom up or from the top down. Others are knit in a modular fashion, but again with little or no sewing.

As we go to press none of our several dozen patterns have seams to sew! Minimal finishing means looking for innovative methods to reduce or eliminate the amount of sewing needed to achieve an attractive finished garment. Knitting in the round with circular needles lends itself to this approach. And knitting from the top, starting with the collar and working down to the bottom edge, means no sewing whatsoever.

Perfect!